BROUGHT TO BED

BROUGHT TO BED

MADELEINE RILEY

With 12 pages of half-tone plates

SOUTH BRUNSWICK AND NEW YORK:
A. S. BARNES AND COMPANY

6925

*Library of Congress
Catalog Card Number 68-24466*

CONTENTS

LIST OF ILLUSTRATIONS

*All illustrations by courtesy of the
'Radio Times' Hulton Picture Library*

ACKNOWLEDGMENTS

ACKNOWLEDGMENTS for permission to use quotations from their books go to the following:

Sir Compton Mackenzie and Macdonald & Co. for *Carnival*; Antonia White and Eyre & Spottiswoode for *The Lost Traveller*; Emyr Humphreys and Eyre & Spottiswoode for *A Man's Estate*; Enid Bagnold and Wm Heinemann Ltd for *The Squire*; Pamela Hansford Johnson and Macmillan & Co. and Macmillan & Co. of Canada for *The Unspeakable Skipton* and *The Impossible Marriage*; C. P. Snow and Macmillan & Co. and Macmillan & Co. of Canada for *Homecomings*; Leonard Woolf and The Hogarth Press for *Orlando* and *Flush* by Virginia Woolf; E. M. Forster and Edward Arnold Ltd for *Where Angels Fear to Tread* and *Howard's End*; Methuen & Co. for *In the Year of the Jubilee, Odd Women* and *Nether World* by George Gissing; Walter Allen and Michael Joseph for *All in a Lifetime*; Doris Lessing and MacGibbon & Kee for *A Proper Marriage;* William Heinemann for *The Forsyte Saga* and *The White Monkey* by John Galsworthy; Macmillan & Co. and the Trustees of the Hardy Estate for *Tess of the D'Urbervilles* and *The Well-Beloved* by Thomas Hardy; the Executors of the late H. G. Wells for *Marriage*; Elizabeth Taylor and Peter Davies for *A View of the Harbour* and *Sleeping Beauty*; Laurence Pollinger Ltd and the Estate of the late Mrs Frieda Lawrence and Wm Heinemann Ltd for *The Rainbow, Sons and Lovers, Women in Love* and *Lady Chatterley's Lover*; Stella Gibbons and Longmans Green & Co. for *Cold Comfort Farm*; Chatto & Windus and Mrs Laura Huxley for *Brave New World* by Aldous Huxley; Field Roscoe & Co. for *Muslin, Esther Waters* and *A Mummer's Wife* by George Moore; Rosica Colin Ltd for *Very Heaven* by Richard Aldington; Rosamund Lehmann and the Society of Authors for *Echoing Grove, A*

ACKNOWLEDGMENTS

Note of Music and *Weather in the Streets*; A. D. Peters & Co. for
Work Suspended and *Brideshead Revisited* by Evelyn Waugh; A. D.
Peters & Co. for *Pursuit of Love* by Nancy Mitford; A. D. Peters &
Co. for *The Judge* by Rebecca West; The Bodley Head for *Ulysses* by
James Joyce and A. L. Rowse and Jonathan Cape for *A Cornish
Childhood.*

INTRODUCTION

IT WAS while lying in bed, a few hours after the first of my five children had been born, when the quality of the pain and the actual nature of the experience were still immediate, that I remembered the chapters in Tolstoy's *Anna Karenina* in which Kitty and Levin's first child is born. I felt that I could testify to the accuracy of the description of Kitty's agonized progress in labour and I wondered if my husband had felt any of Levin's emotions. It then seemed strange that I should identify my experience of childbirth with a fictional account by a man, written in the late nineteenth century, and not with the factual accounts in books like Grantley Dick Read's *Childbirth Without Fear* which I had dutifully read during pregnancy. The fictional account, it seemed to me, had a far greater authenticity (besides being far more interesting). The characters thought about God and Death; in-laws and other people flitted in and out of the bedroom, and, most comforting, no one was very calm or brave.

Lying there I began to remember other fictional childbirths, patriotically limiting my thoughts to those in English novels. I idly allotted marks for accuracy. As I dredged up these scenes, authors' names floated up—what had George Eliot written about childbirth? Surely Mrs Gaskell ought to be able to outdo Tolstoy in describing labour, and yet, even in *Ruth*, I could not recall anything, to make the simplest comparison, as long as Tolstoy's account. What about Maria Edgeworth, the Brontës, Jane Austen? Jane Austen? Impossible to suppose there were any scenes of childbirth in her novels, yet there were births. How did the babies get into the books?

From female novelists I mentally moved along the library

shelves to the male writers. Fielding—I half remembered a woman having a baby in a room where a drunken party was going on in *Tom Jones*, Sterne's *Tristram Shandy*, of course a key novel on childbirth. Smollett? Something about a dream of the devil acting as midwife to a baby which turned into a tennis ball—Dickens, D. H. Lawrence, James Joyce—the names spun round.

From that starting point this book evolved. The choice of authors remains personal and therefore arbitrary. I have, as far as possible, used the authors' own words to build up the picture without cluttering it with my own feelings. In his autobiography, *A Cornish Childhood*, A. L. Rowse says that only two or three books left any imprint on his memory. One of these was *John Halifax, Gentleman*, 'and that I remember for quite the wrong reason—for the extreme sexual excitement I derived from it, from the passage where the wife announces to her husband that she is going to have a baby'.

It would be invidious to deprive anyone of this sort of reaction by superimposing a duller one of my own, so I have left it to the reader to react in his own way to the scenes of fictional childbirth which I evoke.

CHAPTER ONE

SHE DROPP'D HER BURTHEN

'CHILDREN loathe their parents', said Daniel, 'because they can never forgive them the sickening humiliation of birth, the bloody entry into the world, the repulsive captivity of the navel cord.'

Other fictional characters beside Daniel in Pamela Hansford Johnson's *The Unspeakable Skipton*, 1959, take a jaundiced view of childbirth. Gissing in *In the Year of the Jubilee*, 1894, sums up one woman's response to maternity in these words: 'Before her child's coming into the world, she snarled at the restraints it imposed on her; at its birth she clamoured against nature for the pains she had to undergo and hated her husband because he was the intermediate cause of them.'

In *Tom Jones*, by Fielding, published 1749, a retrospective description given by Mrs Fitzpatrick of her labour leaves the reader in no doubt as to the bitterness of her reaction to childbirth:

'I became a mother by the man I scorned, hated and detested. I went through all the agonies and miseries of a lying-in (ten times more painful than the worst labour can be when one endures it for the man one loves) in a desert, or rather indeed, a scene of riot and revel, without a friend, without a companion, or without any of those agreeable circumstances which often alleviate and perhaps sometimes more than compensate the sufferings of our sex at that time.'

Not all fictional confinements are remembered with such horror. In Rosamund Lehmann's *A Note of Music*, 1930, a mother recalls her confinement as being the highmark of her life, a time of transcending happiness, although the birth was painful and dangerous:

> Frequently she spoke of her confinement, her one occasion, her own; measuring time by that supreme event as one should say: Before the birth of Christ or after. Remembering the ten days' rest in bed, the baby, the importance, the ministering district nurse, she smiled dreamily, reliving the miracle of laying down her burden, the bewilderment of pain and joy.
>
> 'When 'e was born', she said, 'the cord was twisted three times round 'is little neck! I nearly lorst him.'
>
> And once she murmured, 'Happiest time of my life it was.'

A romantic affirmation of the joys and beauty of childbirth is made by Meredith in his novel *The Amazing Marriage*, 1895. The heroine has given birth with natural splendour to the satisfaction of the narrator:

> Gower, good fellow, has already gone down to see the young mother three weeks after the birth of her child. She was already renewing her bloom. She had produced the boy in the world's early manner lightly without any of the tragic hovering over death to give life. Gower compared it to a 'flush of the vernal orchard after a day's drink of sunlight'. That was well: that was how it should be. One loathes the idea of tortured women.

But tortured women too can be in tune with Nature. Thomas Hardy in *The Well-Beloved*, 1892, in one of the most beautiful descriptions of fictional childbirth, compares the rhythmic moaning of a woman in labour to the tidal rhythm of the sea. In

2

the novel Pierston, the expectant father, is standing outside his
cottage waiting for the child to be born:

> The sea moaned, more than moaned among the boulders,
> and below the ruins; a throe of its tide timed to regular
> intervals. The sounds were accompanied by an equally
> periodic moan from the interior of the cottage chamber;
> so that the articulate heave of the water and the articulate
> heave of life seemed but differing utterances of the selfsame
> troubled terrestrial Being—which in one sense they were.
> Pierston—for the man in the lane was he—would look
> up from lightship to cottage window; then back again, as
> he waited there between the travail of the sea without, and
> the travail of the woman within. Soon an infant's wail of
> the very feeblest was also audible in the house.

This diversity in English novels in the way the characters
behave and react to childbirth is matched by the variety of
expressions used by authors in order to say that a woman has
given birth. These range from robust, rural-type phrases to
euphemisms which make such an expression as, say, 'The first
fruit of our union' seem quite coarse. Defoe, Fielding and
Smollett, writing in the eighteenth century, use simple, homely
expressions when they write about childbirth. They write, 'She
gave birth', 'She was delivered of a son' or, a characteristic
expression of eighteenth-century novelists, 'She was brought to
bed of a fine boy'.

Defoe has a pithy, evocative phrase, 'She dropp'd her
burthen'.

Other expressions from this period suggest the pain and
effort of birth. Fielding says of a woman about to give birth,
'She was almost ready to cry out', and Scott writes in 1816, in
The Antiquary, 'She took the pangs of travail'.

Scott is an author who uses curious expressions to refer to
childbirth. In two of his novels he employs such idiosyncratic
expressions that the kindest editions of his works elucidate them

in footnotes. In *Guy Mannering*, 1815, when the Laird's wife is in labour, it is observed that 'Clecking time's a canty time', that is, 'Hatching out time is a merry time', or when a woman is in labour everyone should be happy.

'Clecking time' in another of his novels, *Kenilworth*, 1821, is announced by an erudite character saying, 'The lady is even now in Lucina fer opem', which is to say, 'Lucina, do your work', that is, the lady is in labour, Lucina being the goddess in charge of childbirth.

Other nineteenth-century authors use euphemisms out of a desire for delicacy. Some of these expressions are flowery in every sense of the word. George Eliot refers to a death in *Scenes from Clerical Life*, 1858, by this horticultural image:

Her continual langour and want of active interest was a natural consequence of her bodily feebleness and the prospect of her becoming a mother was a new ground for hoping for the best.

But the delicate plant had been too deeply bruised and in the struggle to put forth a blossom it died.

There is no suggestion of the physical process in this as there is in the eighteenth-century expressions. Other sample nineteenth-century novelists, Disraeli, Thackeray and Dickens, also avoid direct mentions of childbirth. Disraeli, in *Henrietta Temple*, 1837, uses the language of a society column, 'Lady Armine presented her husband with a son', and later on in the novel, 'The family circle at Armine has been considerably increased of late, there is a handsome young Armine who has been christened at Glastonbury'.

In Thackeray's novels the ladies do not drop their burthens. Neither the onset of their labour nor its progress is described. In *Vanity Fair*, 1847, George's posthumous child by Amelia makes his first appearance being pressed to his mother's breast:

A day came of almost terrified delight and wonder when the poor widowed woman pressed a child to her breast—

a child with the eyes of George who was gone—a little boy as beautiful as a cherub. What a miracle it was to hear its first cry. How she laughed and wept over it—how love and hope and prayer awoke again in her bosom as the baby nestled there. . . .

A fever and doctors are mentioned later on in this passage, but there is no indication of what has actually happened to Amelia's body.

Of the nineteenth-century novelists, Dickens scores top marks for the most circumspect and unconsciously funny euphemisms. When Dora, the child-wife in *David Copperfield*, 1849–50 (as always incompetent), has a miscarriage, the blood, mess and pain are missed out, the tragedy being broken to the reader in the following way:

> But as the year wore on, Dora was not strong. I had hoped that lighter hands than mine would help to mould her character and that a baby smile upon her breast might change my child-wife into a woman. It was not to be. The spirit fluttered for a moment on the threshold of its little prison, and unconscious of captivity, took wing.

The bird metaphor enables Dickens to refer to Dora's miscarriage without using such a gross word; in *Our Mutual Friend*, 1864–5, he resorts to a nautical metaphor to save himself and his public the embarrassment of using words like pregnancy and labour. Here is how John Rokesmith is told by his wife that she is having a baby and how Dickens announces the birth:

> 'Do you remember, John, on the day we married, Pa's speaking of the ships that might be sailing towards us from unknown seas?'
> 'Perfectly, my darling.'
> 'I think . . . among them . . . there is a ship upon the ocean bringing to you and me . . . a little baby, John.'
> The winds and tides rose and fell a certain number of

times, the earth moved round the sun a certain number of times, the ship upon the ocean made her voyage safely and brought a baby, Bella, home. Then who was so blest and happy as Mrs John Rokesmith saving and except Mr John Rokesmith?

By comparison other Victorian clichés which are used in various novels of the period such as, 'The house received a new inhabitant', 'She gave another child to the household', 'A new person awoke to the light' are straightforward.

Precise language is used in some twentieth-century novels. Some of the nouns used in recent novels when referring to childbirth are 'cervix', 'afterbirth', 'contraction', 'dilation'; the verbs are equally graphic: 'pull', 'push', 'extract', 'torn in two', 'expel', 'bear down'.

All the expressions from novels written in the three centuries are used impartially to refer to the births of sons or of daughters. There the impartiality ends. The reception given to girls and boys born in a selection of three hundred novels leaves no doubt as to which sex is preferred.

CHAPTER TWO

THE WELCOME GIVEN TO
BOYS AND GIRLS

No GIRL reading a selection of English novels can fool herself that she is a member of any but the second sex. The prospective fictional parents, in an overwhelming majority, hope for a boy, and rejoice if they produce a son and heir.

Take a run-in-the-mill novel of the early nineteenth century, *Madeline*, by Amelia Opie, published in 1822. The anxiously awaited-for son and heir has arrived, and in the mother's 'letter', which describes the joy felt by the husband over the baby, a smugness over successfully producing a boy pervades the wife's comments:

> 'It pleased God to spare my life and I am a mother and a nurse and so happy as both. . . . It is a boy and the image of his father! I am so proud of it. . . . Glencarron dares not take it, he is so afraid of letting it fall—but he kisses it and looks at it for minutes together and talks nonsense to it; and sometimes he calls it, and that is so gratifying to me, the little Glencarron.'

Some satisfaction is derived from the name Glencarron being preserved. The chagrin which the couple in Richardson's *Sir Charles Grandison*, 1753–4, experience over the birth of their daughter is also partly due to anxiety over the survival of the family name. The 'female writer' of the news, in the novel, disapproves of their disappointment. Richardson, always careful to take the moral line, evidently thought that to question the Creator's choice of the sex of a child was rather impious:

'Just returned. All happily over. A fine girl! Yet, though a fine one, how are the Earl and his Gertrude disappointed. Poor mortals! how hard to be pleased.'

Most writers have not these pious reservations. Trollope, for instance, shows sympathy for the gentry who value boys more than girls. In an ironical description in *Doctor Thorne*, 1858, he points the contrast between the festivities which take place at the birth of a son and heir and the dearth of rejoicing at the births of his sisters. Admittedly, in this case, quantity as well as quality is a deciding factor in determining the size of the celebrations:

In the first twelve years of their marriage, children came fast into the nursery at Greshamsbury. The first that was born was a boy; in those happy, halcyon days, when the old Squire was still alive, great was the joy at the birth of an heir at Greshamsbury; bonfires gleamed through the countryside, oxen were roasted whole, and the customary paraphernalia of joy usual to rich Britons on such occasions were gone through with wondrous *éclat*. But when the tenth baby and the ninth little girl was brought into the world, the outward show of joy was not so great.

Disappointment over the birth of a girl—to the fictional holder of a title—sometimes takes the form of sour criticism of the wife for not producing a male.

An example of such husbandly rancour is instanced in the laconic letter which Rosalie, the young wife of a nobleman, writes to her ex-governess in Anne Brontë's novel *Agnes Grey*, 1747. As can be inferred from the tone of the letter (meant by the author to be unattractively unfeeling, though the pathetic bravado which comes through puts the reader on Rosalie's side), Rosalie is not repentant over her crime of producing a female child instead of a male, despite her husband's annoyance with her:

> 'I forget whether you like babies; if you do you may have the pleasure of seeing mine—the most charming child in the world, no doubt, and all the more so that I am not troubled with nursing it!—I was determined I wouldn't be bothered with that. Unfortunately it is a girl and Sir Thomas has never forgiven me.'

Rosalie does not pretend to love Sir Thomas: even if she had produced a son and heir she would not have had any satisfaction out of pleasing her husband. In *Leonora*, 1815, by Maria Edgeworth, the loving wife is reported to be in high spirits after she had given birth to a boy because she knew how much her dear husband wanted a son:

> 'Thank God! She is now safe. Her infant to her great delight is a boy; she was extremely anxious to have a son, because Mr L— formerly wished for one so much.'

Not that the preference for a boy is always the pleased acquiescence by a compliant wife with the demands of her husband. In D. H. Lawrence's novel *Sons and Lovers*, 1913, Mrs Morel's joy in having a boy has nothing to do with any wifely satisfaction over pleasing her husband, as he has not expressed any preference, and if he had, this would not have influenced her feelings about the child, as she despises him and his values. When she is told that her child is a boy she is happy on her own account. In her wretchedness and pain she is comforted by the knowledge that she has had a son. This is her own personal female reaction:

> Mrs Morel lay in bed listening to the rain and the feet of the colliers . . .
> She was very ill when her children were born.
> 'What is it?' she asked, feeling sick to death.
> 'A boy.'

And she took consolation in that. The thought of being a mother to men was warming to her heart . . . her love came up hot in spite of everything. She had it in bed with her.

In *The Rainbow*, 1915, also by D. H. Lawrence, the same feminine desire for a son is evidenced in the disappointment of the wife, Anna, albeit momentary, when she gives birth to a girl: 'It was a girl. The second of silence on her face when they said so, showed him she was disappointed.'

Anna's disappointment in having a girl and not a boy sets off in her husband, Will, a strongly protective and possessive love for his daughter. He hates what he counts as disloyalty to the child in Anna's first reaction.

This sort of possessive and protective love which Will experiences for his daughter is felt by Soames in John Galsworthy's *A Man of Property*, 1922. His is a case where extreme possessive love overcomes extreme disappointment over the birth of a daughter. In the novel Soames has married in order to have an heir. The birth of a boy is therefore of the utmost importance for him, so that when, after a complicated labour during which he has had to decide whose life should come first, his wife's or the child's—and he has chosen the child's, influenced by his obsessive desire for a son—when, after all this, the doctor tells him that his child is a girl he feels cheated, swindled. Subsequently his resentment at the wrong sex of the child is swept away by the force of his pride of possession. These, however, are his first thoughts and this is the way in which he behaves before he sees the child:

'What is it?'

'Daughter luckily; a son would have killed her—the head.'

Relief unspeakable and yet—a daughter! It seemed to him unfair. To have taken that risk—to have been through this agony—and what agony—for a daughter! He stood before the blazing fire of wood logs in the hall, touching it with his toe and trying to readjust himself. 'My father,' he thought. 'A bitter disappointment, no disguising it! One never got what one wanted in this life.'

Soames is too disappointed to be able to face seeing his wife and new daughter. He goes to see his father who is dying and there tells him a lie rather than disappoint the dying man by letting him know that the child is the wrong sex. His lie gives the old man great satisfaction:

> 'Good news, dear, good—Annette, a son.'
> 'Ah!' It was the queerest sound, ugly, relieved, pitiful, triumphant—like the noise a baby makes getting what it wants.

Soames and his father's urgent need for a scion stems from their love of their property and possessions, from the desire to hand down to someone of their own flesh and blood what they have accumulated. In *Where Angels Fear to Tread*, 1905, by E. M. Forster, the overwhelming desire of Gino, the feckless Italian husband, for a son is not triggered off by the urge to have an heir to inherit his possessions—for he has none—but by the thought that this will give him a chance to relive himself, an opportunity for personal immortality:

> His one great desire was to become the father of a son like himself and it held him with a grip he only partially understood, for it was the first great desire, the first great passion of his life. Falling in love was a mere physical triviality, like warm sun or cool water, beside this divine hope of immortality: 'I continue.'

Gino is a simple man who is not given to self-examination— he takes his ambition to have a son for granted. The urge to have a son is not confined to the simple. For the introspective intellectual, Lewis Eliot, in C. P. Snow's novel *Homecomings*, 1959, the realization that he wants a boy rather than a girl provokes him into feeling shamefaced about having this desire, but it is as strongly present in him as in Gino. Lewis's friend, Charles March, is also said to want a son; he has been disappointed that all his children are girls. Like Lewis he is apologetic and somewhat uneasy over owning to this preference. In the novel Lewis's wife has been confined at a hospital where she is attended by Charles March, who is a doctor. He telephones Lewis to tell him the news that she has given birth to a boy:

> 'Lewis, is that you?'
> 'Yes.'
> 'You've got a son.'
> 'Are they safe?'
> 'I think they're pretty well.'
> His voice came to me still loud but affectionate and warm.
> 'You've had good luck for once and I envy you.'
> His own children were girls, he had wanted a son and had apologised for it as a piece of Jewish atavism: but he knew that I did too.

How stubborn a preference this is becomes more apparent as more novels are read. A final example may be taken from Evelyn Waugh's novel *Brideshead Revisited*, 1945. In this, the realization that a stillborn child was a girl is said to compensate the father, Rex, for its loss; he would have been more grieved if he had forfeited a son. In this extract his wife, Julia, is retelling the story of her marriage and recounts how she lost her child and how Rex took the news of her death:

> 'I never saw her: I was too ill to know what was going on, and afterwards, for a long time, until now, I didn't want to speak about her—she was a daughter, so Rex didn't so much mind her being dead.'

From the three hundred novels, only three instances can be marshalled in which something like a preference for a girl is felt, one from an eighteenth-century novel, and two from nineteenth-century ones, two by women novelists, and one by a man. Of these only one portrays a person with a whole-hearted preference for a girl, and this preference is evinced not by a father or mother, but by a famously eccentric aunt, a prototype of the wayward English spinster who takes a pride in being a law unto herself; the desire for a great-niece is yet another example of her eccentricity. In the other two stories, in one the wife defends the birth of a daughter while being obliged to note her husband's disdain for females; in the other, the parents are overjoyed with their daughter at once, but it is admitted that they had, during the pregnancy, hoped for a son.

The most militant criticism of the English male's partiality for sons rather than daughters comes from the woman novelist Clara Reeve, in *School for Widows*, 1791. The wife expresses her scorn of her husband's views in tartly sarcastic tones:

> 'Heaven sent me a dear child which I received as its best gift. Strickland was overjoyed at the birth of a son; for he, like other men, wished to continue his family. . . .
>
> The next year I brought forth a daughter who was most welcome to me: but her father set little value upon her. He was one of those *wise* men who thought women a drug and that they were hardly worth rearing.'

Those paragons of parents, Mr and Mrs John Halifax, in Mrs Craik's *John Halifax, Gentleman*, 1856, just scrape into the category of daughter-lovers by the promptness of their joy at the birth of their daughter Muriel: 'It was a girl—I think they had wished for a son; but they forgot all about it when the tiny maiden appeared.'

The outstanding fictional dissenter from those who value boys more highly than girls is, of course, Miss Betsey Trotwood, who appears in Dickens's novel *David Copperfield*, 1849–50. She comes to attend the confinement of her widowed niece and at once instigates a feud with the doctor, Mr Chillip, as she waits downstairs during the birth, with her ears stopped against any noise with 'jeweller's cotton'. Eventually the baby is born and she removes the cotton-wool to question the doctor about the birth. He replies:

'I am happy to congratulate you. All is now over, ma'am, and well over.'

'How is she?' said my aunt.

'Well, ma'am, she will soon be quite comfortable, I hope,' returned Mr Chillip. 'Quite as comfortable as we can expect a young mother to be under these melancholy domestic circumstances. There can not be any objection to you seeing her presently, ma'am. It may do her good.'

'And how is *she*?' said my aunt sharply.

'Ma'am,' returned Mr Chillip, 'I apprehended you had known. It's a boy.'

My aunt said never a word: but took her bonnet by the strings, in the manner of a sling, aimed a blow at Mr Chillip's head with it, put it on bent, walked out and never came back.

Boy or girl, the sex of the baby cannot be known until it is born. In the meantime the fictional parents-to-be are influenced in their behaviour by other speculations. For the unmarried mother, in particular, such considerations are hardly relevant. She has enough to worry about when trying to conceal her condition; she attempts either to prepare for her confinement or to procure an abortion.

CHAPTER THREE

ILLEGITIMATE BIRTHS, INFANTICIDE
AND ABORTION

THE unmarried mothers in this selection are mainly more sinned against than sinning, like Tess in Hardy's novel, who is 'a pure woman', Little Em'ly in *David Copperfield*, who is the victim of an unscrupulous seducer, and like gentle, noble Agnes in Mrs Opie's *Father and Daughter*, who is just too trusting. There are too a few 'sinners', in many ways more attractive heroines than the innocents—Moll in Defoe's *Moll Flanders*, Aphra Behn's devil-may-care *Black Lady*, and Rosamund Lehmann's Dinah in *The Echoing Grove*—all sympathetic characters. The emancipated and the ignorant have, with one or two exceptions, several characteristics and experiences in common. Whatever the circumstances, whether they are raped, seduced or had sexual intercourse willingly, they all end up as unhappy and, in some cases, tragic figures. They feel guilty and ashamed and are generally physically and mentally isolated from their families and friends. Home confinements are rare; most of the confinements are hazardous and take place in unsuitable surroundings.

The most unsuitably placed confinement of an unmarried mother in English novels must surely be the birth of a baby in a fetid crypt among mouldering bones described by George 'Monk' Lewis in his novel *The Monk*, 1795. The unmarried mother in the story is rather exceptional too, for she is a nun who has been seduced by a monk. She remains in her convent during her pregnancy, attempting to hide her condition. Before the nine months are up the nuns have discovered her secret. Whipped up with righteous fury and jealousy they denounce the nun and bundle her into an underground dungeon to starve to death. All this upheaval brings on a premature labour; the nun herself tells the story of the birth and death of her illegitimate child:

'My mental anguish and the dreadful scenes in which I had been the actress, advanced the period of my labour. In solitude and misery, abandoned by all, unassisted by art, uncomforted by friendship, with pangs which if witnessed would have touched the hardest heart, was I delivered of my burden. It came alive into the world: but I knew not how to treat it or by what means to preserve its existence. I could only bathe it with tears, warm it in my bosom and offer up prayers for its safety. I was soon deprived of this mournful employment. The want of proper attendance, my ignorance how to nurse it and the bitter cold of the dungeon and the unwholesome air which inflated its lungs, terminated my sweet babe's short and painful existence. It expired a few hours after its birth and I witnessed its death with agonies which beggar all description.'

Other eighteenth-century unmarried mothers are more fortunate than the nun. Moll, in Defoe's novel *Moll Flanders*, 1722, who is a thief and a prostitute, becomes pregnant either for love or money or both. She is not ashamed of giving birth to her illegitimate children: she is already outside society, beyond the effects of its censure. She does not feel the need to hide her condition, and is described as setting about choosing childbed linen and fixing up help for her confinements with some enjoyment and with a sanguine, untroubled mind. This is Moll, nonchalantly referring to one of her several confinements: 'I was brought to bed about the middle of the day and had another brave boy and myself in good condition as normal on such occasions. My governess did her part with the greatest art and dexterity imaginable.'

Moll's 'governess', a euphemistic title, is a fellow crook, and

'The Little Stranger'—a delicate euphemism

A Second Frontispiece to *Tristram Shandy*—welcome for a boy

her service to Moll is part of their professional association in the criminal city-underworld. Moll is an urban figure.

The mother in Robert Bage's *Hermsprong*, 1796, is a country girl living among honest people, who show her the same easy tolerance with which Moll is treated, only in this case their tolerance does not spring from the communal loyalty of those against the law, but from a feudal habit of mind. In Bage's novel a village girl is having a baby: the father is a gentleman, so the affair is written off as a little mistake but a socially acceptable one. There is no question of the girl being expelled from the community; on the contrary the villagers rally round her with such generous exuberance that their sympathy proves too much for the new mother:

> On the twentieth day of her lying-in she died of kindness and caudle. The young squire had sent in a profusion of the latter and the neighbours had supplied the former, for although the matter was rather a lapse of chastity, or, as they call it, a mishap, yet considering it was a gentleman's child, there was not much harm done.

This cosy home confinement is in contrast to most of the other eighteenth-century illegitimate births which are furtive and take place away from home. Some of these unmarried mothers go into hiding as soon as their pregnancy becomes obvious. In real life there was a good reason for the poor to hide away. Aphra Behn in *The Adventure of the Black Lady*, 1658, explains, with vindictive gusto, why this was. If a girl was identified as being pregnant and about to have an illegitimate child unless 'security to the parish of twenty or thirty pounds' was given, the mother was sent 'by the Overseers of the Poor' to a 'House of Correction and her child to a parish nurse'.

So when a girl's pregnant condition became obvious, if she did not have the necessary money to stop the Overseers from pouncing upon her, her only course was to hide.

In *The Adventure of the Black Lady* Bellamora outwits the

Overseers of the Poor (a patronizing title) who, having heard that she is in an advanced state of pregnancy, want to put her into a House of Correction. Better than just escaping from them, Bellamora's resourceful landlady, who helps her to elude the pursuers, plays a trick on the Overseers and makes them look stupid. This time it is the turn of the respectable to be humiliated. Bellamora keeps her liberty—and her lover, and has the last laugh, for when the Overseers arrive at her lodgings she and her lover have already disappeared out of their reach:

> Whilst they were abroad, came the vermin of the parish (I mean the Overseers of the Poor who eat the bread from them) to search for a young, black-haired lady (for so was Bellamora) who was either brought to bed or just ready to lie down. The landlady showed them all the rooms in the house but no such lady could be found. At last she bethought herself and led them into her parlour where she opened a little closet door and showed them a black cat which had just kittened; assuring them that she would never trouble the parish as long as she had rats or mice in the house, and so dismissed them like the loggerheads as they came.

Fictional unmarried mothers like Bellamora, who defies society, or like Moll, who is indifferent to its rules and standards of behaviour, escape from personal shame and, through having the help of approving friends, are able to accept their illegitimate confinements without distress. In Mrs Opie's *Father and Daughter*, 1801, a pure, innocent and respectable girl also manages to make a partial escape from complete misery and shame, even though she thinks of herself as a disgrace, by her courage and stoicism.

Poor Agnes realizes that she is pregnant and that her lover will not marry her before the child is born:

> When she reflected that she should in all probability be a mother before she became a wife, in a transport of frantic

anguish she implored Heaven in mercy to put an end to her existence.

'O my dear injured father!' she exclaimed. 'I who was once your pride am now your disgrace! and that child whose first delight it was to look up into your face and see your eyes beaming with fondness on her can now never dare to meet their glance again.'

Agnes is confined and proves herself 'superior' to her situation, astonishing the kind woman who helps her during the birth by her 'fortitude and calmness':

The time of Agnes's confinement now drew near—a time which fills with apprehension even the wife who is soothed and supported by the tender attentions of an anxious husband and the assiduities of affectionate relations and friends and who knows the child with which she is to present them, will at once gratify their affections and their pride. What then must have been the sensations of Agnes at a moment so awful and dangerous as this! Agnes who had no husband to soothe her by his anxious inquiries, no relations and friends to cheer her drooping soul by their expressions of sympathy and whose child, instead of being welcomed by an exulting family, must be, perhaps, a stranger to its nearest relations.

But in proportion to her trials seemed to be Agnes's power of rising superior to them, and after enduring her sufferings with a fortitude and calmness that astonished the mistress of the house, whom compassion had induced to attend on her, she gave birth to a lovely boy.

Although it is recorded in the novel that Agnes was not seen to smile after the birth, she is delighted with her child and has 'the natural love of a mother' for her child to offset her sufferings. In Mackenzie's novel *Man of the World*, 1773, there is another unmarried mother who feels this 'natural love'. After a confinement which takes place in the most unsatisfactory conditions—the unmarried mother has only just time 'to send out for the woman who acted as midwife in the neighbourhood'— the child is born. Despite the physical and mental disadvantages of the birth, the mother's natural affection for the child breaks through her misery: 'Distracted as her soul was, this new object drew forth its instinctive tenderness, she mingled tears with her kisses on its cheeks and forgot the shame attending its birth in the natural meltings of a mother.'

Agnes and the unmarried mother in Mackenzie's novel manage to find someone to act as midwife when they start their labour pains, even though they are in lodgings. The mother in Charlotte Smith's *The Young Philosopher*, 1798, is not so well placed. She feels her pains start when she is with a terrible old woman whom she suspects would happily let herself and her child die. She decides that she cannot risk letting the old woman know what is happening; that she must try to appear as though she is not having labour-contractions until she can be with her faithful maid in whom she has confidence. Under the eye of the old woman she forces herself to act the part of someone not in pain, not in labour:

> I was seized with violent pains and could not long doubt of what nature they were. Once assured that my hour was at hand, I determined to bear my sufferings, if possible, in silence, so great was my dread of the old woman in whom I had long accustomed myself to see my murderess and my child's. I know not how in the reduced state I was in I had resolution enough to persevere in the concealment of my pangs: but I did so; and having only my faithful, tender Menie with me, was at two in the morning delivered of a boy.

In another illegitimate confinement in an eighteenth-century novel the mother is also in squalid lodgings but without a 'faithful, tender' maid to help her; in Smollett's *Peregrine Pickle*, 1751, the mother has been obliged to put herself alone to bed in a miserable room in her lodgings. She feels ill and worn out with fatigue and misery:

> Immediately after I had taken possession of my wretched apartment, I was constrained by my indisposition to go to bed and send for the necessary help, and in a few hours a living pledge of my love and indiscretion saw the light tho' the terrors and fatigue I had undergone had affected this little innocent so severely that it scarcely discovered any visible signs of life.

In these examples from eighteenth-century fiction the descriptions of the misery of illegitimate births are set down but not unduly emphasized by the novelists. There is the suggestion inherent in their treatment of illegitimacy that the future can be happy for the unmarried mother after her confinement. The climate of opinion on freedom in sexual behaviour, as reflected in these novels, especially those written by men, is relatively mild. They are not censorious and moral judgements do not take up much space in their books.

The Victorian novelists tend to write of illegitimate births as total tragedies. To conceive a child outside marriage suggests that at least the man, if not the woman too, enjoyed sexual intercourse so much as to run the risk of conception—an idea repugnant to the average Victorian. The unmarried mother is portrayed as an outcast from society. Little Em'ly, in Dickens's *David Copperfield*, 1849, is obliged to emigrate after she has been seduced. Her relations are described as being made broken-hearted by the tragedy. There is no chance that she can resume her normal life, although she is an innocent victim of a sophisticated deceiver. This is an age where novelists write of daughters being turned out into the snow for bringing disgrace on the family. Mrs Gaskell's novel *Ruth* provoked an outcry when it appeared in 1853 by having an unmarried mother as a heroine, and by its shocking plea, albeit heavily qualified, for some tolerance to be shown to the unmarried mother, and especially to the illegitimate child.

In the novel Ruth, an orphan, is taken up and falls in love
with a wealthy, weak young man who seduces her. His domineer-
ing mother finds out that Ruth is pregnant and pays her off with
fifty pounds and an outrageous note in which she accuses
innocent, naïve Ruth of entrapping her son and leading him
into sin. She suggests Ruth should go to 'Fordham Penitentiary':

'... I wish to exhort you', writes the mother, 'to repentance
and to remind you that you will not have your own guilt
alone upon your head but that of any young man whom
you may succeed in entrapping into vice.'

Ruth does not go to the Penitentiary; she is befriended by a
clergyman, Thurston Benson, who takes her home to his sister,
Faith, to stay with them both, before he knows why she is so
miserable. It falls to his sister to tell him the appalling reason for
Ruth's illness and grief:

'Why, Thurston, there is something so shocking the
matter that I cannot tell you.'
Mr Benson changed colour with affright. All things
possible and impossible crossed his mind but the right one.
I said 'all things possible'; I made a mistake. He never
believed Ruth more guilty than she seemed.
'Faith, I wish you could tell me and not bewilder me
with those noises of yours,' he said nervously.
'I beg your pardon; but something so shocking has just
been discovered—I don't know how to word it—she will
have a child. The doctor says so.'

Thurston, whom Mrs Gaskell portrays as being revolu-
tionarily liberal in his ideas on illegitimacy, argues Ruth's case
with his orthodox sister. He has 'been mourning all afternoon
over the sin which has blighted this young creature', nevertheless he insists, despite the gravity of her sin, that Ruth and her
child must be treated kindly.
During the argument Faith refers to the fate awaiting Ruth's

'badge of shame', quoting the case of a certain Thomas Wilkins, another illegitimate child:

> 'The poor, poor child! What it will have to struggle through and endure! Do you remember Thomas Wilkins and the way he threw the registry of his birth and baptism back in your face ... he went to sea and was drowned rather than present the record of his shame.'

Ruth's child, Leonard, does not get himself drowned, but he suffers from his illegitimacy. When he plays with some other children, their father's 'virtuous indignation' is vented on Ruth and he says of Leonard:

> 'That very child and heir of shame to associate with my own innocent children! I trust they are not contaminated.'

Ruth suffers more than ever as the novel progresses, made more vulnerable by her love for Leonard. She has posed as a widow; rumours circulate and she decides to tell Leonard that he is illegitimate:

> 'I did wrong in a way you cannot understand yet' (she saw the red flush come into his cheek, and it stung her as the first token of that shame which was to be his portion through life) '. . . in a way people never forget, never forgive.
>
> '. . . And Leonard,' continued she, in a trembling, sad voice, 'this is not all. The punishment of punishments lies awaiting me still. It is to see you suffer from my wrong-doing. Yes, darling, they will speak shameful things to you, poor innocent child! as well as of me, who am guilty. They will throw it in your teeth through life, that your mother was never married—was not married when you were born.'

Ruth is not allowed by Mrs Gaskell to live down her 'sin' and find normal happiness; she is killed off by a fever (caught when nursing, chastely, her former lover) after enduring heroically a run of trials and humiliations all stemming from Leonard's illegitimacy. Dickens in *Oliver Twist*, published in 1837–8, fifteen years earlier than Mrs Gaskell's revolutionary novel, kills off Oliver's unmarried mother too; she does not have to carry the burden of her shame through a full-length novel, but is mercifully released in the first few pages. Her horrible death in childbirth, attended as she is by a gin-soaked old pauper woman and an uncaringly bored parish surgeon, turns the account into a suitably cautionary one, but there is too in the description more than a hint of Gaskell-like indignation at society's treatment of the unmarried mother. (Dickens in real life had shown some liberality of spirit in his connection with Miss Coutts and Urania Cottage which took in unmarried mothers.)

This is part of the birth of Oliver from *Oliver Twist*. A mysterious, refined-looking young woman arrives exhausted at the gates of the workhouse. She is in labour. During her confinement in the workhouse she is attended by a 'parish surgeon' and an old drunken woman, from the workhouse, who is employed by the parish. The child is born but at first it does not breathe fully but lies

> gasping on a little flock mattress rather unequally poised between this world and the next, the balance being decidedly in favour of the next. Now if during this brief period Oliver had been surrounded by careful grandmothers, anxious aunts, experienced nurses and doctors of profound wisdom, he would almost inevitably and indubitably have been killed in no time. There being nobody, however, but a pauper old woman who was rendered rather misty by an unwonted allowance of beer and a parish surgeon who did such matters by contract, Oliver and Nature fought out the point between them. The result was that after a few struggles Oliver breathed, sneezed and proceeded to advertise to all the inmates of the workhouse

the fact of a new burden having been imposed on the parish, by setting up as loud a cry as could reasonably have been expected from a male infant who had not yet possessed that very useful appendage, a voice, for a much longer space of time than three minutes and a quarter.

As Oliver gave this first proof of the free and proper action of his lungs, the patchwork coverlet which was carelessly flung over the iron bedstead rustled, the pale face of a young woman was raised feebly from the pillow and a faint voice imperfectly articulated the words: 'Let me see my child and die.'

The surgeon had been sitting with his face towards the fire, giving the palms of his hands a warm and a rub alternately. As the young woman spoke he rose and, advancing to the bed's head, said, with more kindness than might have been expected of him:

'Oh, you must not talk of dying yet.'

'Lor, bless her dear heart, no,' interposed the nurse, hastily depositing in her pocket a green glass bottle the contents of which she had been tasting in the corner with evident satisfaction. 'Lor, bless her dear heart, when she's lived as long as I have, sir, and had thirteen children of her own, and all on 'em dead except two and them in the work'us with me, she'll know better than to talk in that way, bless her dear heart. Think what it is to be a mother, there's a dear lamb, do.'

Apparently this consolatory perspective of a mother's prospects failed in producing its due effect; the patient shook her head and stretched out her hand to the child.

The surgeon deposited it in her arms. She imprinted her cold white lips passionately on its forehead, passed her hands over her face, gazed wildly round, shuddered, fell back and died. They chafed her breast, hands and temples; but the blood had stopped for ever. They talked of hope and comfort. They had been strangers too long.

'It's all over, Mrs Thingummy,' said the surgeon at last.

'Ah, poor dear, so it is,' said the nurse, picking up the cork of the green bottle which had fallen out on to the pillow as she stooped to pick the child up. 'Poor dear!' ...

The surgeon leaned over the body and raised the left hand. 'The old story,' he said, shaking his head: 'no wedding-ring, I see. Ah, good night.'

The cost of this confinement is on the parish. To avoid the open shame of a parish-assisted birth, where the control of the mother's and child's future rested with petty officials, it was necessary to find enough money to pay to have the baby privately.

This problem of how to raise the money to hide and have the baby away from familiar surroundings is one which May, the unmarried mother who appears in George Moore's novel *Muslin*, 1884, has to solve. May is worth looking at in some detail, cash worries apart. A typical 'bad girl', vain, selfish and callous, she becomes pregnant and determines that she will not cripple her chances of making a wealthy and respectable marriage in the future by allowing her condition to become obvious among the people in her own town. May's logic is unclouded by sentimentality; she knows that her ambition is to make a socially acceptable, if possible a brilliant marriage, and she knows that to achieve this aim she must appear to be still a virgin or her prospects on the marriage market will be spoilt. Luckily for May, she has a friend Alice, a sweet, good girl who can be relied upon to be discreet. May confides in her and Alice, shocked, but full of pity, advances enough money for May to sneak off to Dublin and have the baby. From the big city May writes to Alice. May's unrefined honesty as revealed in her letters and conversation, her blatant self-pity and selfishness make her a very human character and perhaps more attractive to a present-day reader than Moore intended.

First is an extract from a 'letter' written by May, regaling

Alice with her fears and speculations during her hidden pregnancy:

> 'Isn't it awful to sit here day after day, watching myself and knowing the only relief I shall get will be after such terrible pain. I woke up last night crying with the terror of it. Cervassi says there are cases on record of painless confinements and in my best moments I think mine is to be one of them.'

After the birth May exerts herself to write again:

> 'Just a line—in pencil—I mustn't sit up—to tell you it's all over and all I said was "Thank God, thank God", over and over again as each pain went; it's such a relief, but I mustn't write much. It's such a funny screwed-up looking baby and I don't feel any of those maternal sentiments you read about—at least not yet. And it always cries just when I'm longing to go asleep. Thank you again and again for all you have done for me and been to me. I feel awfully weak.'

Later on: 'Alice heard that the baby was dead, and that a little money would be required to bury it.'

The funeral over and May fully recuperated, she returns jauntily home, unrepentant from a moral point of view, though regretting the inconvenience of having had the child. Sweet, good Alice receives yet another disillusioning shock as May talks breezily about the baby:

> 'Oh, I had such a frightful time of it! If one is married one is petted, consoled and encouraged but alone in a lodging, oh, it was frightful.'
>
> 'And what about the poor baby?' asked Alice.
>
> 'The poor little thing died as I wrote to you, about ten days after it was born. I missed it and felt sorry for it—I really was, but of course, it seems a hard thing to say, but I don't know what I would have done with it if it had lived.'

A situation such as May describes requires some heroism to endure; the furtive pregnancy, the boredom of the waiting period in lodgings, shot through with bouts of fear at the unknown quality of the pain, and finally the birth of an un-wanted child and no awakening of compensatory maternal affection.

The same author who created May, George Moore, does provide a heroine who is an unmarried mother, whose behaviour and emotions are almost the complete opposite of May's, a mother who is irradiated, whose life is transformed, by her love for her child. This is Esther, in *Esther Waters*, 1920. The realistic description of Esther's confinement, which takes place in a large teaching hospital in London, adds authenticity to her agony and humiliation during the birth, and this makes her contrasting joy when she sees her child particularly memorable.

Esther's pregnancy is the result of one of the oldest stock situations, with the class element involved. She is 'taken advantage of' by the cook's son at the house where she is employed as a servant. She is a simple, uneducated girl without pretensions. After the seduction she can no longer continue in her job; she goes off to the city to have her child alone. After some time spent at home, she searches for lodgings and has the good luck to obtain a room, let by a motherly landlady called Mrs Jones, who feels some sympathy for her. It is to Mrs Jones that she goes when her first labour pains begin, to ask her what she should do. The following scene takes place in a warm kitchen: the pains are domesticated by Mrs Jones's calm reassurances. By contrast to the comfort of Mrs Jones's kitchen the later scenes at the hospital appear more frightful. Esther's ignorance of what child-birth is like increases her fear and her pain; Mrs Jones attempts to allay her panic: the pains become more frequent as the time passes:

> 'Hadn't I better go to the hospital yet, Mrs Jones?'
> 'Not just yet, my dear, them is but the first labour pains:

plenty of time to think of hospital: we'll see how you are in a couple of hours.'

'Will it last as long as that?'

'You'll be lucky to get it over by midnight. I have been down longer than that.'

'Do you mind my stopping with you in the kitchen? I feel so frightened when I am alone.'

'No, I'll be glad of your company. I'll get you some tea at once.'

'I couldn't touch anything. Oh, this is dreadful!' she exclaimed as she walked to and fro holding her sides, balancing herself woefully. . . .

At seven o'clock Esther was clinging to the table and with pain so vivid on her face that Mrs Jones laid aside the sausages she was cooking and approached the suffering girl:

'What! is it as bad as that?'

'Oh,' she said, 'I think I'm dying. I cannot stand up, give me a chair, give me a chair!'

Esther has now to leave the refuge of stolid Mrs Jones. The following extracts from Moore's detailed account of Esther's hospital confinement have a dreadful realism. Esther is not a co-operative patient. She arrives at the hospital and goes up the stairs on the arm of an unsympathetic nursing sister. At once she takes a violent dislike to the hospital, the sister and all the staff and to their methods. The bunch of students that Esther encounters are outstandingly callous and insensitive; she is outstandingly prudish and hysterical. Their boorishness, and Esther's hysterical revolt from them, combine to put this description in the front rank of the most disturbing accounts of illegitimate confinements by English novelists. For Esther, to the isolation of being an outcast and to her humiliation, a new horror is added—a sense of physical degradation.

The students, when Esther first sees them, are eating sweets and chatting together. The sight of them fills her with terror: their casualness she interprets as mockery:

> . . . Esther was taken behind a screen by the sister who brought her upstairs, undressed and clothed in a chemise a great deal too big for her, she heard the sister say so at the time, and as she walked across the room to her bed she noticed steel instruments on the round table and the basins on the floor. . . .

> A moment after her pains began again and she saw the young man whom she had seen handling the sweets, approaching her bedside.

> 'Oh, no, not him, not him!' she cried to the nurse. 'Not him, not him! he is too young! Don't let him come near me.'

> They laughed loudly and she buried her head in the pillow overcome with pain and shame; and when she felt him by her she tried to rise from the bed.

> 'Let me go! take me away! Oh, you are all beasts!'

> 'Come, come, no nonsense,' said the nurse. 'You can't have what you like; they are here to learn'; and when he had tried her pains she heard the midwife say it was not necessary to send for the doctor. Another said it would be over in three hours' time.

> 'An easy confinement, I should say, the other will be more interesting.'

Esther's sufferings cover several more pages in the novel. The birth is not in fact easy, but complicated and protracted. Finally she is given chloroform, loses consciousness and the child is born. Now comes the transformation. During the pregnancy and labour Esther has cut a pathetic figure; with the birth of her child a new dignity and authority are invested in her. The boy compensates her, over and above, for all her suffering. He becomes 'her reason for living; not her shame but her triumphant pride'. Her body as well as her mind feels healed by the love she experiences for the child; just as she felt mentally and physically degraded, she now feels both mentally and physically exalted:

> Afterwards the door was thrown open and Esther was wheeled into the passage.
>
> 'Where is my boy?' she said. 'Give him to me.'
>
> The nurse entered and answered, 'Here'. A pulp of red flesh rolled up in flannel was laid alongside of her; it looked at her and her flesh filled with a sense of happiness so deep and so intense that she was like one enchanted. And when she took the child in her arms, she thought she would die of happiness.
>
> She did not hear the nurse speak, nor did she understand her when she took the babe from her arms and laid it alongside on the pillow, saying:
>
> 'You must let the little thing sleep; you must try to sleep yourself.'
>
> Her personal self seemed entirely withdrawn; she existed like an atmosphere about the babe and lay absorbed in this life of her life, this flesh of her flesh, unconscious of herself as a sponge in warm sea water. She touched this pulp of life, and was thrilled, and once more her senses swooned with love; it was still there.

Esther loathes the hospital staff and their maternity service; they do, however, deserve some gratitude from her for preserving her life and that of her child. The extent of her good fortune in having a hospital confinement, repeated examinations and all, can be measured by the account of an illegitimate birth, written a generation or so later than *Esther Waters*, which takes place in *The Echoing Grove* by Rosamund Lehmann, published in 1953.

The baby's death is directly caused by the mother's choice of such an out-of-the-way place to hide during her pregnancy that when her labour pains unexpectedly start the hospital cannot be reached. Dinah is intelligent, emancipated from her conventional background, living a 'free' life. She is capable of making sensible plans for her confinement without being bogged down by guilty regrets:

'I was bound for a private room in the District Hospital; when my time came, I'd be safe there with my layette and wedding ring.'

The situation is, however, tipped towards tragedy, for Rickie is married to Dinah's sister, Madeleine, and the birth must be concealed from her and from the legitimate children of this marriage; it would be too damaging a piece of knowledge for them to bear. Concealment is necessary; Dinah cannot have Rickie with her during the pregnancy; she must manage with some sort of confidante. Her choice, which is narrowed by her unconventional life and views, is unfortunate. Not many women are free enough of responsibilities and inhibitions to accompany a friend to the country to await the birth of an illegitimate child. In Dinah's case the only candidate she can find for the position is an unbalanced Lesbian named Corrigan, likely to prove treacherous because of her mental and emotional instability (she does, in fact, betray the lovers). She is the type of person fated to be mixed up only in disasters. Dinah and Corrigan take possession of a remote cottage and there Dinah begins her labour prematurely. It is winter, the roads are blocked with snow and the hospital cannot be reached:

'What a grotesque disaster; all of a piece with the rest. All of a piece to stay in an isolated cottage at the bottom of a Cornish lane in winter when you're eight months pregnant.'

There is nothing for it, Corrigan has to act as midwife. Dinah gives birth and as she lies back exhausted she hears Corrigan's voice:

'Oh! . . . It's not breathing.' Puzzled, matter-of-fact. Not a tactful thing to remark in that tone of voice to a woman

Moll Flanders—a happy-go-lucky unmarried Mother

Hetty in Prison—a case of infanticide

just through labour. Before that with my eyes fast shut, I'd
seen her, Corrigan, pick it up out of the tumbled bed. 'It's a
boy.' Just what I'd expected to have: three normal words.
I felt my huge smile flood through me, burst out of my
spent body like the huge irradiated backwash of the final
wave of birth. A boy. Under my shut eyes I listened,
peacefully waiting for what was only to be expected—the
sound of new-born crying. I wasn't worried by the silence;
in all those hours I hadn't had a moment's fear, and, bound
to me in our reality, nor had she. I was travelling first class
and taking her along for the privileged hell of it: wild
country but *de luxe* conditions. Poor old Corrigan, she'd
never done anything in style, she thought we were initiating
her. We bamboozled her. She was an old clown doing her
damnedest, born to the game, condemned to it, assiduously
tumbling in the ring; we were the glamorous artistes doing
the new sensational trapeze act high among the lights with a
roll of drums. Breathtaking acts, drama and suspense.
Danger? Not for such star performers.

Her movements creaked, breathed round me while a
timeless age went by. 'It's dead, I think.' Flat statement.
My lids lifted, she was holding him up. I saw his blood-
stained human head. She'd cut the cord and tied it: she was
clever with her hands. One couldn't say she'd lost her
head. . . . It was just bad luck. Or it had gone on too long,
we'd thrown our hands in without telling one another that
we knew the game was up. Thinking back afterwards, I
realized there was a moment about half way through when
the intimation reached me that . . . something biding its
time from the beginning had stepped from an ambush and
taken charge. The enterprise was moving to a predestined
outcome. But one is never prepared for what one has
prepared to bring about. Her bulky figure blocked the
low-ceilinged room, solid between the lamplight dying on
the table and pewter snowlight through the pane. Dawn.

Some time in the small hours the blizzard had drawn ahead of *me*, and emptied itself out. There was a cry then animal, and it was mine. It trailed its length out of the window and died in the nine-days-hanging shroud of the dead world.

Dinah wanted the baby. She loved its father and had happily planned her future round the child: together they would live an idyllic life abroad visited as often as possible by Rickie. The still-birth is a tragedy for her. Esther's maternal love and Dinah's grief are natural emotions. There are some fictional unmarried mothers who not only fail to have such natural feelings about their children, but who act towards them in the most unnatural way possible. Infanticide is not an easy subject for a novelist, but an analysis of the unhappy state of mind of an unmarried mother who kills her child is bravely made by an early novelist, Mrs Inchbald, in her book *Nature and Art*, 1796, with some success:

> Deep contrition for past offences had long been the punishment of unhappy Agnes, but till the day she brought her child into the world, remorse had been averted. From that day, life became an insupportable load, for all reflection was torture. To think, merely to think, was to suffer excruciating agony, yet never before was thought so intrusive: it haunted her in every spot, in all discourse or company: sleep was no shelter—she never slept but her racking dreams told her—she had slain her infant.
>
> They presented to her view the naked innocent whom she longed to press to her bosom while she lifted up her hand against its life. They laid before her the piteous babe whom her eyeballs strained to behold once more while her feet hurried her away for ever.

'Contrition', 'remorse' are words which describe private emotions, but infanticide is not a private affair of conscience. It is a capital crime for which the law must prosecute. If the mother can be proved to have done the murder herself, the law is simple to apply; if, on the other hand, she does not actually kill the child herself, but has put herself in a position where she is during her confinement with people of a 'dubious' character who 'do away with the child', the guilt of the mother is debatable, the just verdict less easy to be reached. In Scott's *The Heart of Midlothian*, 1818, a case of suspected infanticide of this nature is brought to court. The girl, Effie Dean, who is accused, is a girl of previous good character; until she became pregnant she mixed only with respectable people—then she was driven to mix with criminals recommended by her lover. The corrupt and criminal are the only ones to whom she can turn now she is 'in trouble'; they offer to 'help out', a phrase which covers all kinds of sinister practices—from the selling of children to the killing of them. An extract from a 'speech' made in court during the trial scene, from the novel, provides the particular background to the circumstances under which the child 'disappeared'. Effie:

'instead of resorting when her time of travail approached, to the protection of her own family, was induced to confide herself to the charge of some vile agent of this nefarious seducer, and by him conducted to one of the solitary and secret purlieus of villainy, which to the shame of our police, still are suffered to exist in the suburbs of the city, where with the assistance and under the charge of a person of her own sex, she bore a male child, under circumstances which add treble bitterness to the woe denounced against our original mother. . . . The unfortunate young woman was visited by a fever incidental to her situation. In this fever she appears to have been deceived by the person that waited on her, and, recovering her senses, she found she was childless in that abode of misery. Her infant had been carried off perhaps for the worst of purposes by the wretch that waited upon her.'

Despite the Defence Counsel's efforts, the girl is found guilty of infanticide (the sentence is not carried out, the rest of the book being devoted to a narration of the efforts of Effie's gallant sister, who, after a series of adventures, manages to obtain an acquittal).

In George Eliot's *Adam Bede*, 1839, Hetty, a girl who has actually murdered her child, is found guilty and sentenced to death (though she is reprieved at the last moment). Hetty is too simple and naïve to be classed as a deliberate criminal. She is not a villainess; her faults before the crime have been of a minor order. She is vain, frivolous and irresponsible, nothing more. When she gets caught up in a situation which terrifies her—that of being pregnant and with no prospect of the man marrying her—she loses all rational control. Her motive for killing the baby is not vindictive: she kills the child to attempt to get back to normality—she just wants to go home, for life to go on as before. She has been seduced by a well-to-do, sensual and cowardly man, who drops her as soon as he knows that she is pregnant and that she expects him to marry her. Terrified by her abandonment Hetty does not confess to her doting aunt and uncle what has happened; instead she runs away. Without the slight comfort of a bed in one of those 'solitary and secret purlieus of villainy' available to the Scottish city girl, Hetty gives birth.

The corpse of the baby, which she has abandoned to die, is discovered, and Hetty is identified as its mother and brought to court. In a pathetically simple speech afterwards she gives her explanation of how the idea came to her to leave the baby to die:

'And then the little baby was born when I didn't expect it: and the thought came to my mind that I might get rid of it and go home.'

Hetty in prison talks about how she felt and what she did to the child:

'I seemed to hate it—it was like a heavy weight round my neck; and yet its crying went through me, and I daren't look at its little hands and face.'

She wanders about carrying the baby until she sees a hole under a nut tree like a little grave and it darts into her mind that she could 'lay the baby there and cover it with grass and the chips. I couldn't kill it any other way. And I'd done it in a minute; and oh, it cried so, Dinah—I couldn't cover it quite up. . . .'

'To get rid of' an illegitimate baby by murdering it and then go home does not work out as poor Hetty discovers. The unmarried mother who takes an alternative course of 'killing' the child in embryo by procuring an abortion does not run Hetty's risk of losing her life through the processes of justice. (She may lose her life, incidentally, because, as the operation is illegal, it is more likely to be performed by either unqualified or ignorant people than by a doctor with scruples and a good reputation.) Nevertheless these risks apart, and given a 'good address' and sufficient money they can be overcome, a girl can have an abortion and take up her former place in society. But, as three sample novelists show, to terminate a pregnancy illegally is not easy, and if her former place in society is still there the girl who has had an abortion is not the former person that she was.

Olivia, in Rosamund Lehmann's *The Weather in the Streets*, 1936, becomes pregnant while having an affair with a married man. Wretchedly sick she pretends to her cousin, Etty, that she has had a letter from a friend:

'She's been having an affair with some man or other, I believe, and to her horror she finds she's started a baby.'

'Oh, my dear, how *shattering*!'

Was it imagination—one rapid, questioning glance from Etty?

'She wants to know if I can help her.'

Etty reflected seriously: 'Has she tried pills?'

'She doesn't say. There are pills, are there? That really work? She'd try anything, I'm sure. Do chemists sell them?'

'I know of one who does. But I've never heard of them working if it's really the worst. . . . They may, of course.'

Etty fell silent, adding, 'They give you the most *stupefying* diarrhoea, that I do know. . . . Still, she might try.'

. . . .

'Has she got any money?'

'No . . . but I think . . . she says she could get some—a little—I don't know how much—from the man perhaps.'

'I do know someone . . .' said Etty uncertainly.

'In London?'

'Yes, let me think . . . his name . . . it's ages since I . . . Tredeaven—that's it.'

'Is he in the telephone book?'

'Oh yes. He's a what d'you call it—manipulator or something. . . . He's got a more or less respectable practice. This is a *side*-line.'

'How could I get hold of him? Could I ring up and make an appointment for her? Or take her to see him?'

Etty was silent.

'He won't take anyone unless he knows who's sent them,' she said at last. 'You see, it's *fearfully* dangerous for him. If you're caught it means prison. . . . In spite of his being, of course, a public *benefactor*. I suppose he's saved *regiments* of unfortunate *erring* women from *ruin*. . . .'

'You mean', said Olivia, 'he might refuse to do it—if she just went out of the blue?'

Silence again.

'You could give my name, I suppose. . . .' Etty stirred. Her slightly protruding eyes between curly doll's lashes became fixed with a certain wild blankness on her cousin. 'Only it was so long ago . . .'

'Did you go to him, Ett?'

'My dear, *once*. Wasn't it *shattering*?' The colour came

up in her fragile egg-face, painfully, from neck to brow. She laughed, rather shakily. 'The *wages* of *sin*, darling.'

Olivia cannot make up her mind straight away to go to the abortionist. Time passes as she stagnates in London:

She was no longer so thin: it must be growing, getting enough nourishment. Her breasts hurt. She fancied her figure changing perceptibly. When do one's clothes begin to get too tight? . . . She remembered Kate, unfamiliar and touching in a grey maternity frock with white ruffles. 'Such dignities will not be for me. To be rid, to be rid, to be rid of this . . . to be not sick . . . I should be hanging on doors, lifting wardrobes and pianos, trying to fall downstairs, doing everything I can. . . .'

Olivia goes to the abortionist finally.

'Don't worry, Mrs Craig, we'll fix you up.'

'Thank you so much. . . .' She fidgeted with her bag. 'And about—I'm not quite sure—what it is you charge—about your fee. . . .'

'My fee is a hundred'—Mr Tredeaven crossed his knees —'pounds, not guineas,' he added with a reassuring smile.

'I see.'

Silence fell heavily . . . a body blow . . . Mr Tredeaven took up his fountain-pen from beside the blotter, unscrewed it, turned it about, replaced the top.

'It's a bit difficult,' she said. Her heart beat thickly. What did I imagine? Twenty at the outside. Has the emerald put my price up?

He tapped his nose with his pen.

'Well, I don't want to be hard on you,' he said at last. 'Say eighty.'

. . . .

'Thank you very much.' For his tone suggested magnanimity. 'When do you want it? Before? Now?'

'No, no, no.' He chided gently. 'Come, come now, tact,

dear lady!... There's no such desperate hurry.' He opened his appointment book. 'Suit you to bring it with you when you come?'

'Yes, I could do that.'

He said suavely: 'Preferably not a cheque, if you don't mind.'

'Notes?'

'If it's not giving you too much trouble. Just in an envelope, you know.'

'All right, I'll do that. On Friday at three then.' She got up.

'Friday at three.' He too rose. He held out his hand; strong, plump, manipulative fingers with cushiony tips.

'Is it painful?' she said.

'What a lot of worries!' He shook his head, chiding again, paternally, half playfully, still holding her hand.

'I'm not afraid. I only wanted to know.'

'You needn't worry,' he said. 'Don't think about it. A few days taking it easy afterwards and your troubles will all be over.'

The abortion is performed on the Friday:

'Stay where you are, Mrs Craig,' he said softly. 'There now. Quite comfy? That's right. Don't worry. All over. Wasn't too bad, was it, eh?'

'No, thank you.'

He put a cushion under her head, threw a light rug over her. She lay flat on the hard surgical couch and closed her eyes. Several tears ran down her face and dried there.

'Relax, Mrs Craig.'

Mr Tredeaven tells Olivia that the bleeding will start later on. By chance her ex-husband is with her when it does begin and he calls a doctor who gives her some pills. She lies in bed eating, sleeping and bleeding. Her lover whom she eventually tells about the abortion turns out to be very glad that she did not keep the child as he is about to become the father of a legitimate child.

Olivia has to find out the safe address (a difficulty also described by Penelope Mortimer in *Daddy's Gone a-Hunting*), negotiate with the abortionist, and recover as best she can from the physical and emotional shock without her lover's help. In Emyr Humphreys's novel *A Man's Estate*, 1955, the emotional disturbances in a girl's mind who is about to have, and after she has had, an abortion, are also described with feeling. She is better placed than Olivia to have the operation. She is financed by the father of the unborn child, Wally, who fixes up all the details of finding a doctor willing to perform the operation. He drives her from their home town, sees the doctor with her, settles the bill willingly. The girl has merely to submit to the simple operation—but just how degrading this is, and what a grave effect it has on the girl, can be judged from the following excerpt:

'You know my fee?' I heard him say to Wally. 'Come this way please.'

I lay there trembling while he put on a white overall and scrubbed his hands in a wash basin. He talked to me with his back turned.

'Now this is a simple operation. You have nothing to fear. No pain. Just a little discomfort. I shall explain it to you so you can co-operate intelligently. Do you understand?'

'Yes,' I said.

'Take hold of this,' he said. 'Relax. Forget about me. Breathe this as you need it; keep it on your face. Analgesia. Do you understand?'

He kept asking me if I understood. 'You will bleed,' he said, 'of course that is necessary. Don't be frightened. It's perfectly normal.' Bleeding. Bleeding. Bleeding. 'I shall

ring up the hospital,' he said. 'They will take care of you
for a few days. For safety's sake. A moment, please.'

I heard him telephone. 'Ah, doctor, good morning. I
have a woman here. She is bleeding rather badly. . . . Never
mind, never mind.' I heard him ringing again. 'Hello,
Camiton Hospital. The house surgeon, I want to speak to
the house surgeon. . . . Ah, good morning, doctor, I have a
woman here, she is bleeding rather badly.'

He rang up four times before he turned to Wally.

'All right, Mr Francis. Take her to Breadfather Street
Hospital. Thank you. She will be admitted. She might have
to stay for a few days. It's a good hospital. No, don't say
anything. Just take her in. Routine, very simple.'

I was sick and sick of myself. Bleeding. Bleeding.
Bleeding. Weak. Tired. Glad to be where someone did not
know me. Glad Wally had gone. Sick of him asking, 'Has it
stopped?' Sick of his anxiety. Why should he worry? In
bed, alone and silent I didn't speak not even to the nurse. I
wanted to be alone for ever.

One clear fact emerges from these descriptions of the termina-
tion of illegitimate pregnancies as from the others quoted,
whether they deal with illegitimate births, or infanticide or
abortion. In all of them it is the woman who is punished for
having extra-marital relationships—by Nature and by society,
not the man. The disparity of the effect on the fictional men and
women who have conceived a child outside the bonds of marriage
is great. 'Why should he worry?'

Perhaps the most notorious case of the disproportion of
suffering and guilt between a man and a woman who has an
illegitimate child is that of Tess in Thomas Hardy's *Tess of the
D'Urbervilles, A Pure Woman*, 1891. In the preface to the fifth
and later editions Hardy wrote about the success of his novel:

> . . . it was quite contrary to avowed conventions that the
> public should welcome the book and agree with me in

holding that there was something more to be said *in fiction* than has been said about the shaded side of this well-known catastrophe.

What Hardy does say is compassionate; the tone of the writing amplifies the sense of injustice.

Tess has been raped. As one of the villagers says of the child: 'A little more than persuading had to do wi' the coming o't, I reckon.'

Tess looks after her baby, feeding it herself:

'She's fond of that there child though she mind pretend to hate en and say she wishes the baby and her too were in the churchyard.'

The baby dies in infancy: Tess meets, falls in love with and marries Angel Clare who worships her for her purity. On their wedding night he confesses to 'eight and forty hours' dissipation with a stranger'.

In a chapter entitled 'The Woman Pays' Tess in turn asks Angel to forgive her for her lapse from purity; she tells her story and says to Angel:

'Forgive me as you are forgiven! *I* forgive *you*, Angel.'
'You—yes, you do.'
'But you do not forgive me?'
'O, Tess, forgiveness does not apply to the case. You were one person; now you are another.'

Angel leaves Tess unable to bear the sight of her. She atones for her 'sin' in the end by murdering her seducer and forfeiting her own life.

Hardy's tragedy is extreme: like Mrs Gaskell's *Ruth*, his novel is a protest against society's treatment of an unmarried mother. In a far less over-weightedly militant novel than Mrs Gaskell's, and in a far less sombre story than Hardy's, E. M. Forster makes the same plea for tolerance. In his novel *Howards End*, 1908, he exposes, with precision, the double standard applied by society to the parents of an illegitimate child. In Forster's novel one of two intellectual, liberal-minded sisters is about to have an illegitimate child. Her pregnancy is the result of intercourse with a clerk of intellectual aspirations, whom the sisters had be-friended, and for whom Helen temporarily felt responsible and sorry. Helen realizes, and Forster remarks simply on her realization, that she must take it for granted that 'Society would henceforth exclude her'. To conceal her pregnancy from her family and friends, Helen goes abroad. She is inveigled back into England and tricked into a meeting with her sister Margaret, who, seeing Helen's condition, feels great sympathy for her. Margaret, who is married to a conventional man, Henry Wilcox, is obliged to tell him that Helen is pregnant; it is not possible for the sisters to conceal the fact. Margaret asks that Helen should be treated with love and kindness. Henry, after blustering that her 'seducer' must be horse-whipped, replies:

'Helen commands my sympathy,' said Henry. 'As your husband I shall do all for her that I can, and I have no doubt she will prove more sinned against than sinning. But I cannot treat her as if nothing had happened. I should be false to my position in Society if I did.'

The smug obtuseness of this speech arouses Margaret's fury. It is especially distasteful because Henry was unfaithful to his first wife, and Margaret, who inadvertently found this out, had forgiven him and married him without recriminations. Now she attempts to force him to see how unfair his attitude to Helen is, in the light of his own past:

'You shall see the connexion if it kills you, Henry! You have had a mistress—I forgave you. My sister has a lover—you drive her from the house. Do you see the connexion? Stupid, hypocritical, cruel—oh, contemptible! A man who insults his wife when she is alive and cants with her memory when she is dead. . . . Only say to yourself "What Helen has done, I've done". The two cases are different? You have betrayed Mrs Wilcox, Helen only herself. You remain in Society—Helen can't. You have had only pleasure—she may die.'

Helen's story has only to be compared with, to take one random example from Victorian fiction, the lot of the girl in Jerome K. Jerome's *Three Men in a Boat*, 1889, to show that some progress has been made towards establishing a more liberal, humane and realistic approach in novels to the unmarried mother and her illegitimate child since the nineteenth century. Jerome's summary of what a girl could expect in the way of treatment if she became pregnant while unmarried is prompted in the story by the corpse of a young woman being fished out of the river. The reason for her suicide is revealed in the following way, in an episode entitled 'A rather hackneyed story'.

We found out the woman's story afterwards. Of course it was the old, old, vulgar tragedy. She had loved and been deceived—or had deceived herself. Anyhow she had sinned—some of us do now and then—and her family and friends, naturally shocked and indignant, had closed their doors against her.

Left to fight the world alone, with the millstone of her shame around her neck, she had sunk even lower and lower. For a while she had kept both herself and the child on the twelve shillings a week that twelve hours' drudgery a day procured her, paying six shillings out of it for the child, and keeping her own body and soul together on the remainder.

Six shillings a week does not keep body and soul together very unitedly. They want to get away from each other when there is only such a very slight bond as that between them; and one day, I suppose, the pain and dull monotony of it all had stood before her eyes plainer than usual, and the mocking spectre had frightened her. She had made one last appeal to friends, but, against the chill wall of their respectability, the voice of the erring outcast fell unheeded; and then she had gone to see her child—had held it in her arms and kissed it, in a weary dull sort of way, and without betraying any particular emotion of any kind, and had left it, after putting into its hand a penny box of chocolate she had bought it; and afterwards, with her last few shillings, had taken a ticket and come down to Goring.

She had wandered about the woods by the river's brink all day and then, when evening fell and the grey twilight spread its dusky robe upon the waters, she stretched her arms out to the silent river that had known her sorrow and her joy. And the old river had taken her into its gentle arms, and had laid her weary head upon its bosom, and had hushed away the pain.

Thus had she sinned in all things—sinned in living and in dying. God help her! and all other sinners, if any more there be.

Jerome's attitude, which he seems to feel is reasonably tolerant, appears by the side of Hardy and Forster self-righteous and patronizing. A contemporary novelist could not now write, without laying himself open to ridicule, of an illegitimate child as being 'a millstone of shame' (just to put this phrase beside Isherwood's description of Sally Bowles's abortion or any passage from a recent novel, *The L-Shaped Room* by Lynne Reid Banks, 1960, in which an unmarried mother keeps her baby, having triumphantly come to terms with her situation, is to reveal the extent of the progress away from the earlier attitude), but it would be wrong to dismiss this description and the many like it, from eighteenth- and nineteenth-century English novels as being melodramatic and implausible. Their accuracy can be measured against a real life official directive which was made when a new 'lying-in hospital' was opened in 1767. This stated that 'single, pregnant women' were to be given beds in the hospital, even though they were unmarried 'such as are deserted and in deep distress' and the reason given for their admittance was 'to save them from Despair and the lamentable Crimes of Suicide and Child Murder'.

The assumption implicit in this directive that a bed in a hospital will save an unmarried mother from despair and suicide leads to speculations about the sort of influence, its power and its quality, which the medical profession can and does exert on women giving birth to legitimate as well as illegitimate children. From English novels the picture which emerges of doctors and midwives and the way they behave during childbirth, while it does not suggest that they actually intentionally cause despair and thoughts of suicide in their patients, certainly does not suggest that they induce mental peace and happiness in the women in their charge.

CHAPTER FOUR

DOCTORS AND MIDWIVES

THERE flashed into Chris's mind, the description of his first
accouchement, given him by a medical student who still
seemed a little shell-shocked by the experience. The waves
of pain accompanied by groans and cries, the good-
natured cynical doctor tying a sheet to the bed and saying
cheerfully 'Pull, Mother!' the whiff of chloroform, the
extraction of a small apparently par-boiled hairless ape, the
mess—the smell. . . . A most impressive physical reality if
you like, but beautiful? Marvellous?

This extract is from *Very Heaven* by Richard Aldington
which was published in 1936. If it had been written a hundred
years earlier or twenty years later, most of the details would
have been different. The changes in the practice of midwifery in
English novels (both in who practises it and in how it is prac-
tised) in the last two and a half centuries have been radical. For
instance in Aldington's picture of a typical confinement, the use
of an anaesthetic, the presence of the medical students, the
doctor being in charge not the midwife, are all comparatively
modern innovations and would not be found in earlier accounts.
In novels written some years later than Aldington's the chloroform mask has been replaced by a gas and air apparatus, and the
bearing-down sheet whisked away on the tide of the Natural
Childbirth movement.

Already the sheet on the bed-end seems old-fashioned to be
mentioned in a novel written in the 1930's. The sheet was used

Midwife going to labour—with her Brandy

Mrs Gamp proposes a toast—in Gin

so that the mother might add to the pressure of her contractions by pulling on some material and so enable herself to bear down more strenuously. Lawrence, in *Women in Love*, 1922, also refers to this practice. He describes a newly carved piece of sculpture which depicts a woman 'sitting naked in a strange posture and looking tortured, her abdomen stuck out. The young Russian explained that she was sitting in childbirth, clutching the ends of the band which hung from her neck, one in each hand so that she could bear down and help labour'.

Lawrence and Aldington refer to the continuation of this practice, H. G. Wells to a 'special sort of needle', James Joyce to the 'twilight sleep', Scott to the persistence of 'puerperal fever' and Sterne to the 'newly invented forceps'; from English novels many of the most dramatic changes in obstetrics may be traced. Novelists give startling information about the new techniques used to deliver a baby, and about changes in the conditions tolerated in hospital and home confinements. The drop in infant and maternal mortality rates, as a result of anti-septics and the introduction of pain-blurring anaesthetics, is marked by a diminishing number of fictional deaths in child-birth. What is also shown up, with subtlety and accuracy, in novels is the shift in the social status of the doctor and mid-wife, and the change in their relationship to one another and to the mother—perhaps the most interesting aspect and certainly the one about which the novelist, who is not hampered by having to exercise the discretion required of the medical profession, is able to reveal some strange facts.

The English novel which gives the fullest information of the 'art of obstetrics' is *Tristram Shandy*, 1760–8, by Lawrence Sterne. When Sterne was writing *Tristram Shandy* a revolution in the practice of midwifery was taking place. The 'newly invented forceps', which had been devised by the Chamberlen family, had been brought over to England and publicized by the man-midwife, Smellie. These forceps had changed the whole manner of tackling a difficult delivery. Hence, in the novel, Dr

Slop's delight in his new tools and Mr Shandy's great interest—
anything to do with childbirth fascinates him. He has the
greatest enthusiasm for studying the contemporary techniques
of delivery, and in particular that of the Caesarean operation.
Mr Shandy has read well and widely about childbirth and has
some alarming information. During his course of reading he
displays a spontaneous and irreverent interest in this medical
information, which he interprets and criticizes for himself with
no feeling of there being any possible inferiority in his views to
those of the medically qualified authors. Nothing is too abstruse
for his scrutiny and evaluation.

What really holds a grip on his imagination is the Caesarean
operation; Shandy is very much in favour of this way of extracting the child from the womb and decides that it is a more
desirable method to use than letting the child be born in the
normal way. He reaches this conclusion after he had read just
what happens to the child and to its brain as it makes its way out
of the mother, buffeted by her strenuous contractions. He has,
to his horror, found out that

> . . . the lax and pliable state of a child's head in parturition,
> the bones of the cranium having no sutures, at the time,
> was such—that by force of the woman's efforts, which in
> strong labour pains was equal upon an average to the
> weight of 470 pounds avoirdupois acting perpendicularly
> upon it—it so happened that in 49 instances out of 50 the
> said head was compressed and moulded into the shape of an
> oblong conical piece of dough, such as a pastry cook
> generally rolls up in order to make a pie of. Good God,
> cried my father, what havoc and destruction must this make
> in the infinitely fine and tender texture of the cerebellum! Or
> if there is a juice, as Borri pretends, is it not enough to make
> the clearest liquid in the world feculent and mothery?

The more Mr Shandy reads on, the more he becomes con-
vinced that the normal method of delivering a child is wrong,

inviting as it does squashed-headed infants to be born with damaged brains. Better than letting the head be born first, and so be subjected to the greatest pressure, is to extract the baby by its feet—a breech birth; still safer is for the mother to be delivered by Caesarean section. This idea takes root in Mr Shandy's brain to Mrs Shandy's horror:

The incision of the abdomen and uterus ran for six weeks together in my father's head; he had read and was more than satisfied that the wounds in the epigastrium and those in the matrix were not mortal; so that the belly of the mother might be opened extremely well to give passage to the child. He mentioned the thing one afternoon merely as a matter of fact to my mother; but seeing her turn pale as ashes at the very mention of it . . . he thought it as well to say no more of it—contenting himself with admiring what he thought of no purpose to propose.

Mrs Shandy's alarm is justified when it is remembered that the first successful Caesarean operation in Great Britain, when both the mother and the baby were saved, was in 1738, *Tristram Shandy* being published in 1768—and that this remained for some time an isolated case. (It did not, in fact, become a safe operation until the twentieth century.) Baulked by his wife's terror from ordering a Caesarean section from Dr Slop, Mr Shandy compromises by deciding on a breech birth. With the help of the new forceps the child must be persuaded to come feet first so that the head will be protected from the first crushing shock of birth. Mr Shandy has in Dr Slop a great ally; he was 'the fittest of all for my father's purpose'—that is Mr Shandy's—'for though the newly invented forceps was the armour he had proved and what he had maintained to be the safest method of deliverance yet, it seems, he had scattered a word or two in his book in favour of the very thing which ran in my father's fancy tho' not with a view to the soul's good, in extracting by the feet, as was my father's system—but for reasons merely obstetrical'.

The eighteenth-century doctor's technical resources were few—beside the forceps, Slop's pride, he has little else to help him in treatment of a woman in childbirth but a knife and his hands. This 'man of science' does not carry anything in his 'green baize bag' for the comfort of the mother, to alleviate her pain. The only panacea mentioned is a bottle of julap—a spicy, cordial stimulant—and that is broken. It is not Slop's concern to try to relieve pain. Anaesthetics had still to be discovered.

That there was no general use of drugs to obliterate the pains of childbirth is true, yet there is a mention in an eighteenth-century novel of a drug being administered during childbirth which made the mother unaware of her pains. It is a strange case, the motive for using the drug being not a compassionate but a sinister one. It is not used to increase the chances of the mother's survival by eliminating the shocks of pain. On the contrary, the midwife who dopes the mother in Charlotte Smith's *Count de St Geran* in her *Romances from Real Life*, published in 1787, has made a most unprofessional agreement to kill the baby as soon as it is born. In order to carry out the murder without detection she wants to make the countess, the mother in question, unconscious so that there will be no witness of the killing. She puts the mother out of consciousness with an unspecified, powerfully effective drug (in fact the murder does not come off; she bungles the job, and only injures the child's head):

> The unfortunate Countess, now left in the hands of the cruel woman whose interest was to deprive her of her child, was delivered of a son while totally unconscious of the birth, the draught given her by the midwife having reduced her to a state so near resembling death that she no longer knew what befel her. As soon as the infant was born, the midwife prepared to destroy him. . . .

Obviously this was an exceptional case and an exceptional drug. When, in the middle of the nineteenth century, ether and then chloroform were found to be safe anaesthetics, it quickly became common practice for anaesthetics to be used in midwifery. The first use was in 1847; soon it was available for the rich and poor in childbirth, and fictional mothers began breathing it in; Gissing in *Odd Women*, 1893, writes of a Mrs Widdowson from the slums being given chloroform by the doctor during childbirth (this does not prevent her from dying, however). The discovery of anaesthetics did not bring in an era of painless childbirth in novels. Mothers continued to scream with pain as they gave birth. This was so because a dose of chloroform sufficiently large to obliterate pain at the same time causes the mother to lose consciousness completely, so that she is unable to co-operate with the midwife's instructions during labour. Consequently it was, and is, in England, generally administered, if at all, only in the final stage of labour, so the fictional mothers still endured hours of agony.

When, in 1912, Compton Mackenzie wrote of childbirth in his novel *Carnival* he portrayed the mother during labour as being painracked and miserable, and he commented: 'There was not much to make the great adventure of childbirth endurable.'

The midwife's sole contribution to making the mother comfortable was to 'go down and boil some milk' for a hot drink. In the same novel Mackenzie describes another harrowing confinement, only at the end of which, after hours of pain, is chloroform administered and Jenny, the mother, mercifully loses consciousness. The pains are violent: 'Jenny's great thought was that never again would she endure this agony if but this once she were able to survive it.'

No drugs are offered during the 'agony' until almost at the end of the confinement, when she is finally given chloroform. She groggily comes to only after the child has been delivered:

> Jenny knew little more until, recovering from the chloroform, she perceived a candle, large as a column, burning with a giant, spearhead flame and beyond the blue and silver lattice, Jenny apprehended a fuss of movement.

'What is it?' she asked in momentary perplexity.

'Tis a boy,' said Mrs Trewhella. 'A grand lil' chap.'

A compromise method of offering chloroform in small but frequent doses, results in some alleviation of the pains, when given throughout the most painful stages of labour, without the patient losing all sense of what is going on. Unlike those women who are given chloroform in the final stage of labour, these mothers are able to participate consciously in the actual birth. The method, giving a 'twilight sleep' as it was called, became famous when it was first used in England during one of Queen Victoria's confinements. Sir James Clark, writing of giving chloroform to Queen Victoria, remarked: 'It was not at any time given so strongly as to render the Queen insensible.'

The pain was lessened and the queen stayed awake. But by 1922 this method was still not universally used in the British Isles except for the wealthy *élite*. So that Mr Bloom, in James Joyce's *Ulysses*, 1922, remembers a forceps birth lasting three days, during which time the woman's only comfort was a vinegar compress on her forehead. In recalling this confinement he refers to Queen Victoria's better luck in being able to have her whiffs of chloroform to ease her pains:

'Sss Dth, dth, dth! Three days imagine groaning on a bed with a vinegared handkerchief round her forehead, her belly swollen out: Phew! Dreadful simply! Child's head too big; forceps. Doubled up inside her trying to butt its way out blindly, groping for the way out. Kill me it would. Lucky Molly got hers over lightly. They ought to invent something to stop that. Life with hard labour. Twilight sleep idea. Queen Victoria was given that. Nine she had. A good layer.'

The feeling that 'they ought to invent something' to ease the pains of childbirth was not shared by everyone. The partial achievement of this aim by the use of ether, chloroform and 'the twilight sleep' met with a strong reaction from people who felt it was unnatural to have anaesthetics used during childbirth and therefore that it was undesirable. This conflict is demonstrated in *The White Monkey* by Galsworthy, 1929, in which Fleur, an expectant mother who is frightened of what her confinement will be like, is being reassured by her husband Michael. When he points out that she will have a 'twilight sleep' and, as he blithely but inaccurately forecasts, escape all pain, Fleur has doubts as to whether she ought to accept the chloroform.

> 'Ducky, you'll have a twilight sleep and know nothing about it and be as right as rain in no time.'
> Fleur freed her hand.
> 'Not if it's no good for him. Is it?'
> 'I expect so, sweetheart. I'll find out. What makes you think——?'
> 'Only it's not natural. I want to do things properly.'

Fleur's mistrust of the 'twilight sleep' is based on the idea that pain was natural, and that if it was avoided some unnatural consequence would result. Her mistrust of the idea of 'twilight sleep' does not arise from religious feelings; but this suspicion that it was not right or proper to dodge pain was held by many religious people who based their objections on theological arguments. Their views were expressed in such statements as: 'Chloroform is a decoy of Satan, apparently offering itself to bless women, but in the end it will harden society and rob God of the deep, earnest cries which arise in time of trouble for help.'

An instance of this theory that the pains of childbirth were ordained by God as right and necessary, and that it was thwarting His purpose to try to put an end to a woman's sufferings in childbirth by anaesthetics, is given by H. G. Wells in his novel *Marriage*, 1912, in which he portrays the doctor as having 'a lingering *theological* objection to chloroform'.

On the heels of this objection to anaesthetics has come the rejection of anaesthetics on the grounds that their use cheats, not God, but the mother, if she loses consciousness, of the unique experience of birth—that is the theory of Natural Childbirth. The vehemence of the opposition to the theory, and the proud conviction of the 'natural' mother of its veracity, are epitomized in the following brief exchange from *The Unspeakable Skipton* by Pamela Hansford Johnson, published in 1959, between Dorothy, a notable 'natural' mother, and Daniel, 'the Unspeakable Skipton', who does not hesitate to proclaim publicly his distaste for maternal boastings of the joys of childbirth:

'Your myth of the beauty of maternity', he continued, 'makes me want to vomit. Were you ever present at the birth of a single one of your children, or were you full fathom five under ether?'

'Do excuse me,' said Mathew with a sick, polite smile as he slipped away.

'I studied relaxation,' Dorothy retorted proudly, though she was scarlet up to the hair line. 'I was a natural mother.'

The conditions under which fictional mothers like Dorothy give birth are deliberately unnatural in their sterility. When towards the end of the nineteenth century Lister discovered the way to prevent the spreading of infection, by the washing of hands with carbolic soap and then the rinsing of them in a basin containing carbolic acid, the whole practice of midwifery was changed. The applying of the antiseptic principle by doctors and midwives, the new emphasis on scrupulous cleanliness in maternity work, results in the scrubbed sterility of the twentieth-century fictional confinement. The contrast between the births before this discovery and its application and after it is very great. Before the use of antiseptics, puerperal fever, which was passed by the ill-washed hands of doctors and midwives from mother to mother, was responsible for the deaths of thousands of mothers and infants. The results of this infection, and of the generally unsterile conditions in which babies were delivered, are mirrored in the frequent tail piece to so many fictional confinements of the eighteenth and nineteenth centuries. Such as: 'Mrs Squeeze lay of a dead child; she herself languished a few days and died' (from *The History of Mr Bragwell* or *Two Wealthy Farmers* by Hannah More, 1795).

A distressing description of a mother and child dying as a result of puerperal fever is included by Sir Walter Scott in his novel *St Ronan's Well*, published in 1824. The fatal results of the fever were so well recognized that when the mother, Annie, in her last moments is visited by a Lord Etherington, he agrees to come to the makeshift bed of this unfortunate creature, but he says as a matter of fact:

> 'I am afraid I can be of little use to a poor woman in a childbed fever.'
>
> 'Puerperal, my lord, puerperal,' said Lady Penelope.
>
> Lord Etherington was now standing beside the miserable flock bed, in which lay the poor patient, distracted in what seemed to be her dying moments, with the peevish clamour of the elder infant, to whom she could only reply by low moans, turning her looks as well as she could from its ceaseless whine to the other side of her wretched couch, where lay the unlucky creature to which she had at last given birth; its shivering limbs imperfectly covered with a blanket, its little features already swollen and bloated, and its eyes scarce open, apparently insensible to the evils of a state from which it seemed about to be speedily released.

As the nineteenth century progressed novelists like Dickens and Disraeli drew attention to the dangerously insanitary conditions in which childbirth took place. Both, interested in social conditions, had in childbirth descriptions an ideal vehicle for displaying the sufferings of the poor. The cramped, filthy room where the mother gives birth in *Sybil*, written by Disraeli in

1845, gives an appalling indication of what the 'beautiful experience of childbirth' could be like in the nineteenth century:

> With the water streaming down the walls, the light distinguished through the roof with no hearth even in the winter, the virtuous mother in the sacred pangs of childbirth gives forth another victim to our thoughtless civilization; surrounded by three generations whose inevitable presence is more painful than her sufferings in that hour of travail; while the father of her coming child, in another corner of the sordid chamber, lies stricken with typhus which his contaminating dwelling has breathed into his veins and for whose next prey is perhaps destined his new-born child.

The confinement of Mrs Dorrit, as described by Dickens in *Little Dorrit*, 1857, also brings into focus the atrocious conditions under which the poor in those days were expected to give birth. There could be no greater contrast to the hygienic hospitals of today, staffed by rubber-gloved, be-masked midwives working in labour rooms equipped with shining drums of sterile dressings and immaculate linen, than 'the labour ward' in *Little Dorrit*, a fly-infested room in the Marshalsea prison, equipped with fly-traps of vinegar and sugar, and with cabbage leaves on hand for use by the charwoman who has been promoted for the occasion to a nurse:

> In the debtors' confined chamber Mrs Bangham, charwoman and messenger . . . had volunteered her services as fly-catcher and general attendant. The walls and ceiling were blackened with flies. Mrs Bangham, expert in sudden device, with one hand fanned the patient with a cabbage leaf, and with the other set traps of vinegar and sugar in gallipots, at the same time enunciating sentiments of an encouraging and congratulatory nature adapted to the occasion.
>   'The flies trouble you, don't they, my dear?' said Mrs

Bangham. 'But perhaps they'll take your mind off it and do you good—what between the burying ground, the grocers', the stables and the paunch trade, the Marshalsea flies get very large. P'raps they're sent as a consolation if we'd only known it. How are you now, my dear? No better? No, my dear, it ain't to be expected; you'll be worse before you're better and you know it, don't you? Yes, that's right! And to think of a sweet little cherub being born inside the lock. Now ain't it pretty, ain't that something to carry you through it pleasant? Why, we ain't had such a thing happen here, my dear, not for I couldn't name the time when. And you a crying too?' said Mrs Bangham to rally the patient, more and more. 'You making yourself so famous! With the flies a falling into the gallipots by the fifties! And everything going on so well. And if here ain't your dear gentleman along with Dr Haggage.'

Wretched conditions such as these encouraged the high infant and maternal mortality rates. The decline in the deaths of mothers and babies in the twentieth century is due, in part, to the abolition of insanitary conditions. The other reasons for the drop in deaths at childbirth are the advance in the technical skills of the doctors and midwives, the employment of anaesthetics and antiseptics, and the antenatal care which is now a recognized routine.

The mothers in eighteenth- and nineteenth-century novels do not visit their doctors during their pregnancy. Most of the references to what happens during this time are about 'childbed linen', which could, it seems, be very expensive. An instance of how much an eighteenth-century mother would be prepared to spend on baby clothes is given by Defoe in *Colonel Jack*, 1722. The Colonel baulks at the size of the bill his wife is proposing to incur and insists on her cutting down the cost:

I told her as to her child, which she called her burthen, it should be no burthen to me, as to the rest she might do as she pleased, she might however, do me this favour, that I should have no more lyings-in at the rate of 136L at a time, as I found she intended it should be now.

After the birth a bargain is finally struck:

She was content during her lying-in to abate a little, tho' it was but a very little indeed, of the great expense she had intended; and with some difficulty and persuasion was content with a suit of childbed linen of 15L instead of the one she had intended of three-score.

Godwin, in his novel *Fleetwood*, 1805, does not give the details of price, but merely stated that 'a cradle and a chest of childbed linen' are bought, and in 1872 George Eliot in *Middlemarch* refers to 'embroidered robes and capes' as being the sole equipment which had been collected for the baby whose premature birth occurs during the novel.

But not all prospective parents in English novels escape from their doctors and midwives, and from the buying of medical supplies during the nine months. In *Work Suspended* by Evelyn Waugh, published 1941, the prospective father Roger becomes overwrought from the incessant medical care and attention which are being focused on his wife Lucy, who is expecting their first child. The quantity of goods which it is decided by the midwife must be bought, leads him to conclude that antenatal care is overrated. He has more than the price of 'childbed linen' to pay out for and worry over:

'It's all this damned pre-natal care,' said Roger. 'Do you realise that maternal mortality is higher in this country than it's ever been? D' you know there are cases of women going completely bald after childbirth. And permanently insane. It's worse among the rich than the poor too?'

Miss Meiklejohn said: 'Lucy is being wonderful. She doesn't realise.'

The nurse occupied herself with extravagant shopping

lists. 'Does everyone have to have all these things?' Lucy asked, aghast at the medical and nursery supplies which began to pour into the house. 'Everyone who can afford them,' said Sister Kemp briskly, unconscious of the irony. Roger found some comfort in generalising.

'It's anthropologically interesting,' he said, 'all this purely ceremonial accumulation of rubbish—like turtle doves brought to the gates of the temple. Everyone according to his means sacrificing to the racial god of hygiene.'

It is significant that in this extract from *Work Suspended* it is Sister Kemp who is described as being the one to make out the shopping lists and it is to her that the mother goes when she wants to ask any questions. She is obviously a figure of authority —a professional woman.

The midwives in the eighteenth- and nineteenth-century novels are very different types. In real life in the eighteenth century the midwives were the object of a notorious public dispute. They were under fire for their incompetence, charged with causing two-thirds of the deaths among women and infants because of 'the want of due skill and care in those women who practise the art of midwifery'. What made the dispute so acrimonious was that the attack came from doctors or 'men-midwives', who were competing for the first time in the field of midwifery, which up to then had been the province of women alone. When Defoe and Sterne were writing their novels, in which they refer to doctors and midwives, the quarrel between the two sexes was hot. The men claimed to save lives with their new instruments and techniques, the women insisted that there was no need for the presence of men at a confinement, that a midwife could deliver a child without their help and with more skill; and they defended themselves against the charges of incompetency drawn up against them by the men-midwives in a series of pamphlets.

The pamphlet war gave such notoriety to the name 'man-midwife' that it became the vogue for these doctors to call themselves 'accoucheurs', hence Dr Slop's insistence in *Tristram Shandy* on being called an 'accoucheur'. It could not be denied that, whatever the men called themselves, with their invasion into the field of obstetrics the infant and maternal mortality rate decreased.

So it is no wonder that the shrewd and well-off woman, the *Fortunate Mistress*, in Defoe's novel of the same name, published as early as 1724, was already making sure that there was a qualified man on call in case there were any complications during her labour or the lying-in period. She is not content to trust herself, without this provision, to the sole care of women. She authorizes her maid, Amy, to engage a fair-sized staff ready for her confinement, not only a midwife and a nurse at a good salary, but also another woman assistant and the services, if it proved necessary, of a man-midwife who would be on hand in an emergency:

> . . . she got an English midwife and an English nurse to come over, on purpose to attend an English lady of quality, as they styl'd me, for four months certain: the midwife, Amy had agreed to pay a hundred guineas to, and bear her charges to Paris and back again to Dover, the poor woman who was to be my nurse had twenty pounds, and the same term for charges, as the other.
>
> I was very easy when Amy return'd and the more because she brought with the midwife a good motherly sort of woman who was to be her assistant and would be very helpful on occasion and bespoke a man-midwife at Paris too, if there should be any necessity for his help.

The 'man-midwife controversy' was very fierce by the time Sterne was writing *Tristram Shandy*, 1770–8. Mr Shandy, as an up-to-date man, is determined to have a man-midwife, Dr Slop, and that he shall be in charge. The midwife is there solely to placate Mrs Shandy. As in real life, Slop and the midwife, as representatives of the two sides of the 'war', do not work as a team. They are rivals. They observe no professional etiquette in their dealings with each other. Each despises the other and expects and hopes they will make a fool of themselves. On the evidence which Sterne provides the incompetence of the mid-wives cannot be refuted:

'. . . the child is where it was,' continued Susannah, 'and the midwife has fallen backwards upon the edge of the fender and bruised her hip as black as your hat.'

The man-midwife, Slop in this case, it would appear had still a good deal to master of the technique of delivering a child, but he is less conservative than the midwife. He has a pioneer's relish for his job; he burbles excitedly to Mr Shandy:

'It would astonish you to know what improvements we have made of late years in all branches of obstetrical knowledge but particularly in one single point, of the safe and expeditious extraction of the foetus. . . .

Sterne's comedy is heightened by the real-life incompetence in childbirth methods which was revealed in the midwife versus man-midwife row. The use of forceps, which was one of the topics by which the strongest feelings and words in the quarrel were aroused, is satirized in the report that Slop 'with his vile instruments' has crushed the baby's nose in pulling it out into the world. (However, he proved himself a 'man of science' by soon being found 'making a false bridge with a piece of cotton and a thin piece of whalebone out of Susannah's stays to raise it up'.)

Slop and the midwife are harmless comedians. They are funny without being sinister. The mother and child survive the ordeal of being their patients. (If a death did occur when they were on a case it would surely be as a result of over-enthusiasm —perhaps a failure when experimenting with a new method, or the unfortunate result of a female demonstration of the superiority of some old-fashioned technique.)

But Dickens's doctors and midwives are death ridden; they are sinister as well as being comic; being quite heedlessly ignorant and neglectful of their patients. They are unqualified and without social status. In his portrait of Mrs Gamp in *Martin Chuzzlewit*, 1843, and her friend Mrs Harris, Dickens created a symbol of the worst type of district nurse who was employed among the poor. Callous, drunkardly and unscrupulous, Mrs Gamp is the archetype of the uncaring and uneducated midwife.

The following monologue by Mrs Gamp, in which she relates the difficulties of a midwife due to the unreliability of her clients over commencing labour at the time predicted, pinpoints by the language and style of speech attributed to her the low social status of a nineteenth-century midwife:

'Mrs Gill', I says, 'was never wrong with six and is it likely, ma'am—I ask you as a mother—that she will begin to be irreg'lar now? Often and often have I heard him say I says to Mrs Harris, meaning Mr Gill: that he would back his wife agen Moore's almanack, to name the very day and hour for ninepence farden. Is it likely, ma'am, I says, as she will fail me this once?' Says Mrs Harris, 'No, ma'am, not in the course of nater. But,' she says, the tears a-fillin in her eyes, 'you know much betterer than me, with your experience, how little puts us out. A Punch's show,' she says, 'a chimbly sweep, a newfoundland dog or a drunkin man a-comin round the corner sharp, may do it.'

What Dickens did to ridicule the unprofessional midwife who relied upon drink, cunning and old wives' tales, by creating Mrs Gamp, he did too for untrustworthy doctors who took on childbirth cases, when he drew the portrait of the 'gone-to-seed' doctor in *Little Dorrit*, 1857, who appears with the fly-catching Mrs Bangham in the confinement scene. In the filthy room already referred to, these two practise the art of obstetrics, keeping going during the long labour by drinking steadily from a shared bottle of brandy. They are a team united only by their

Tea party when viewing the new baby—an occasion for old wives' tales

Credulity, Superstition and Fanaticism—The Litter of Rabbits

common thirst and the crass insensitivity of their manner to their patient, Mrs Dorrit. Passing the bottle to and fro between themselves they attempt to deliver the child. In the following extract the doctor's appearance and his 'professional' conduct are described:

The doctor was amazingly shabby in a torn and darned rough weather jacket out at the elbows and eminently short of buttons (he had at one time been the experienced surgeon carried by a passenger ship), the dirtiest white trousers conceivable by mortal man, carpet slippers and no visible linen.

'Childbed,' said the doctor. 'I'm the boy!' With that the doctor took a comb from the chimney piece and stuck his hair upright—which appeared to be his way of washing himself—produced a professional chest or case, of the most abject appearance, from the cupboard where his cup and saucer and coals were, settled his chin in the frowsy wrapper round his neck and became a ghastly medical scarecrow.

This is the extent of his preparations apart from ensuring that some brandy is on hand. Mrs Dorrit's labour progresses slowly and painfully while the doctor under the transparent cover of great concern for the 'nurse', Mrs Bangham's health and strength lasting out the ordeal, splits the brandy with her:

Mrs Bangham submitted, and the doctor having administered her potion, took his own. He repeated the treatment every hour, being very determined with Mrs Bangham. Three or four hours passed and the flies fell into the traps by the hundreds, and at length one little life hardly stronger than theirs, appeared among the multitude of lesser deaths.

'A very nice little girl indeed,' said the doctor, 'little but well formed. Hulloa, Mrs Bangham! You're looking queer! You'll be off ma'am, this minute and fetch a little more brandy, or we shall have you in hysterics.'

These rogues have little in common with Waugh's Sister Kemp except they too employ a facetious, jollying-on way of talking to the expectant father and the mother-to-be. Mrs Bangham's arch plea to Mrs Dorrit to cheer up and 'think of a sweet little cherub being born inside the lock. Now ain't it pretty, ain't that something to carry you through it pleasant?' is in the same strain of whimsy that Sister Kemp uses to refuse a second drink:

> 'The fathers need nearly as much care as the mothers,' said Sister Kemp. 'No, not another, thank you, Mrs Simmonds, I've got to keep in readiness, you know. It would never do if baby came knocking at the door and found Sister unable to lift the latch.'

In Enid Bagnold's *The Squire*, published 1938, the expectant mother is spoken to in quite different tones from the Bangham-Kemp ones, but then her relationship with her midwife and with her doctor is different, for it is that of a disciple to his masters. She makes a joyful sublimation of her mind and body to their wishes and commands. The Squire is an early 'natural' mother: the complete co-operation demanded by this method of child-birth between the doctor and midwife and the mother gives her intense satisfaction. Her surrender to the wills of the doctor and midwife is utterly willing, and so deeply felt that it is described as being a spiritually satisfying relationship. So much so that the 'Squire' calls the doctor and midwife 'the monk' and 'the nun'.

In Miss Bagnold's novel the Squire is expecting her seventh child. She savours her pregnancy. Bound up in anticipation the only people who ultimately matter to her as the time draws near for the birth are 'the monk' and 'the nun'. Her acceptance of the central belief of the Natural Childbirth movement is brought out in a conversation which she has with a friend just before the baby is due to be born, in which she attempts, by metaphorical comparisons, to show that childbirth need not be a painful experience if it is approached in a positive way: if the mother gives her full co-operation to the doctor and midwife, and to the contractions and impulses of her own body:

'Perhaps childbirth turns into pain only when it is fought and resisted? I'm aching. I'm restless. I can't tell you how. But there comes a time, after the first pains have passed, when you swim down to a silver river, running like a torrent, with the convulsive, corkscrew movements of a great fish, threshing from its neck to its tail. And if you can marry the movements, go on with them, turn like a screw in the river and swim on, then the pain . . . then I believe the pain becomes a flame which does not burn you.'

The birth is natural, but the Squire accepts some help from anaesthetics towards the end of her labour, during which she has implicitly, and with pleasure, obeyed the doctor and midwife. In the following passage the elevated, priest-like quality of the role of this twentieth-century doctor and midwife during a 'natural birth' is demonstrated by the use of ecstatic, figurative prose':

The monk and the nun were about her bed, acutely directed on her, tuned to her every manifestation. With eyes fast shut she lent herself to their quiet directions, clinging to the memory of her resolve that when the river began to pull she would swim down with it, clutching at no banks. With a touch of anaesthetics from a gauze mask to help her she went forward. Her mind went down and lived in her body, ran out of her brain and lived in her flesh. . . . Now the first twisting spate of pain began. Swim then, swim with it, for your life. If you resist, horror and impediment. If you swim, not pain but sensation! Who knows the heart of pain, the silver, whistling hub of pain, the central bellows of childbirth which expels one being from another. None knows it who, in disbelief and dread has drawn back to the periphery, contracting the will of pain, braking against inexorable movements. Keep abreast of it, rush together, you and the violence which is also you! Wild movements, hallucinated swimming. Other things exist than pain.

It is hard to gauge pain. By her movements, by her exclamations she would have struck horror into anyone but her monk and nun. She would have seemed tortured, tossing, crying, muttering, grunting. She was not unconscious but she had left external life. She was blind and deaf to world surface. Every sense she had was down in Earth to which she belonged, fighting to maintain a hold on pain, to keep her pace with it, not to take an ounce of will from her assent to its passage. It was as though the dark river rushed her to a glossy arch. A little more, a little longer. She was not in torture, she was in labour; and she had been thus before and knew her way. The corkscrew swirl swept her shuddering until she swam into a tunnel—the first seconds of anaesthesia.

Now the shocked and vigorous cry of the born rang through the room. From its atavistic dim cradle, from a passage like death, crying with rage, resenting birth, came the freed and furious cave child coated in mystery, the heavy-heeled, vulnerable young, the triumph of the animal world, the triumph of life.

Now out of her river the mother was drawn upwards, she became the welcomed, the applauded, the humoured. Faces smiled over her.

'What is it?' Nine months of wondering in one second solved.

'A boy, a beauty.'

The doctors and midwives in these novels, apart from this quiet-voiced, dedicated pair, are not edifying figures. Their professional standards are low, their treatment of their patients insensitive, their conduct suspiciously incompetent. No wonder Dr Grantley Dick Read, in his book *Childbirth Without Fear*,

1942, condemns the novel as being one of the chief promoters of fear in his women patients, though in fact he is not referring to any of these unsavoury medical characters when he makes his complaint, but to descriptions of labour itself; he takes exception to all the screams and moans issuing from the pages of novels. He cites several novels, by men and by women authors, as among the chief offenders. But it is female novelists who have popularly a bad name for terrorizing their readers by piling agony upon agony. However, a selection from confinement scenes by women novelists, including some descriptions where the sheets are thrown back and all exposed, and others where the reader's ingenuity is taxed to find out if a baby has been born during a discreet chapter, suggests that there is more than one extreme when women get down to writing about women in labour.

CHAPTER FIVE

WOMEN IN LABOUR

'You remember Rosamund Dobson at school?'
    'Only too well. When we were about twelve she told me
that when one has a baby one's stomach bursts open'—
Tory threw her hands apart—'and has to be stitched up
again afterwards.'
    'Well, Geoffrey is her son.'
    'Then I hope he was born in the normal way. She must
have been pleased and surprised.'

If the Rosamund Dobson referred to in this conversation
from Elizabeth Taylor's *A View of the Harbour*, 1947, had read
a couple of novels by contemporary women novelists, she would
not have had to wait for the birth of her son Geoffrey to find
out about childbirth; she would have known what goes on when
a baby is born from the first contraction to the expulsion of the
afterbirth.

    Perhaps though it was just as well that she had not turned to
novels as reference books. Nancy Mitford in her novel, *The
Pursuit of Love*, 1945, has put on record how disturbing the
study of childbirth can be for girls of school age, when the text-
books used are fictional. The girls in Miss Mitford's novel have
not found out the physical facts of childbirth until 'remarkably
late'. They have a characteristic feminine fascination for the
subject; a compulsion to uncover every fact that they can which
derives from the half-horrifying thought that this is something
which is probably going to happen to their own bodies in the
future. The hair-raising account which Linda unearths is not a

comfortable vehicle for self-identification, and the girls seek
reassurance from Aunt Sadie, mother of seven; her personal
reminscences, however, are hardly less alarming:

Last holidays our great obsession had been childbirth on
which entrancing subject we had been informed remarkably
late, having supposed for a long time that a mother's stomach
swelled up for nine months and then burst open like a ripe
pumpkin shooting out the infant. When the real truth
dawned upon us it seemed an anti-climax until Linda
produced, from some novel, and read out in ghoulish tones,
the description of a woman in labour.

'Her breath came in great gulps—sweat pours down her
brow like water—and can this face, twisted with agony, be
that of my darling Rhona—can this torture chamber really
be our bedroom, and this rack our marriage bed? "Doctor,
doctor!" I cried, "do something"—I rushed out into the
night' . . . and so on.

We were rather disturbed by this, realising that too
probably we in our turn would have to endure these
fearful agonies. Aunt Sadie, who had only just finished
having her seven children, when appealed to, was not very
reassuring.

'Yes,' she said vaguely, 'It is the worst pain in the
world. But the funny thing is you always forget in between
what it's like. Each time when it began, I felt like saying,
"Oh now I remember stop it, stop it," and of course by
then it was nine months too late.'

At this point Linda began to cry and say how difficult it
must be for cows, which brought the conversation to a
close.

Miss Stella Gibbons also makes fun of lurid childbirth
descriptions in novels, especially novels written by women. Her
summary of the different types of childbirth descriptions is
introduced by Flora, the heroine of *Cold Comfort Farm*, 1932,

who is reflecting that, as with so many women who have had no personal experience of childbirth, she has derived her information about childbirth from novels—in particular those written by women. She make an astringent assessment of what she has read:

> She had a lively acquaintance with confinements through the works of women novelists, especially the unmarried ones. Their descriptions of what was coming to their less fortunate married sisters usually ran to four or five pages of close print or eight or nine pages of staccato lines containing seven words and a great many dots arranged in threes.
>
> Another school dismissed confinements with a careful brightness, a 'So-sorry-I'm-late-darling-I've-just-been-having - a - baby - where - shall - we - go - for - supper - afterwards?' sangfroid which Flora, curiously enough, found equally alarming.
>
> She sometimes wondered whether the old-fashioned though doubtless lazy method of describing the event in the phrase 'She was brought to bed of a fine boy' was not the best way of putting it.

One point which is made by Stella Gibbons in this *Cold Comfort Farm* selection of childbirth descriptions is valid and noteworthy; that is when she draws attention to what she terms the 'old-fashioned' way of referring briefly to the event by some such phrase as 'She was brought to bed of a fine boy'. The case-book detail, from enema to afterbirth, with which some women novelists now refer to childbirth is a very recent development. This is what makes the accounts by contemporary women novelists so exciting. They are new. Today, for the first time, a woman novelist has the social freedom to exploit her fundamental advantage of having had first-hand experience of childbirth by writing, without evasion, of what happens to a woman's body and to her mind when her child is being born.

Women novelists of the eighteenth and nineteenth centuries

writing about childbirth seem to be careful to avoid direct mention of anything physical. As one reads through a batch of novels of this period written by women, the omission of child-birth references becomes very apparent. Modesty, it appears, is the watch word. These ladies write of men and women falling in love and getting married, but they do not then follow this up with a chapter on childbirth.

Take Jane Austen's six novels. They are all domestic in subject. In four of them children are born, but all these births are 'off-stage'—the reference to them is passing. In *Sense and Sensibility*, 1811, the birth is introduced into the novel by way of a newspaper announcement: 'Within a few days after this meeting, the newspapers announced to the world that the lady of Thomas Palmer, Esq. was safely delivered of a son.' (In a reported account of an illegitimate birth in the same novel the actual birth is not mentioned, but there is a reference to the event in which the words 'lying in' and 'delivery' are used.)

In *Emma*, 1816, one of the principal characters, Mrs Weston, has a child. Her pregnancy and labour are not mentioned, and that she has had a baby is observed in one discreet sentence: 'Mrs Weston's friends were all made happy by her safety: and if satisfaction could be increased more, it was by knowing her to be the mother of a little girl.'

Mansfield Park, 1814, contains the brief comment: 'She was preparing for her ninth lying-in.'

In *Northanger Abbey*, 1818, there is the nearest to any emo-tional response to childbirth, a brief amusement on the part of the novelist at the frequent pregnancies which she ascribes to Mrs Morland, the mother of the heroine of the novel, Catherine: 'She had three sons before Catherine was born and instead of dying in bringing the latter into the world as anyone might expect, she lived on—lived to have six children yet', and again, referring to Mrs Morland's fertility, 'Her time was so much occupied in lying-in'.

That this avoidance of direct childbirth mentions and scenes is not just a freak trait of a spinster novelist can be demonstrated by reference to the work of a few other early novelists who were married as well as single. So, for example, Fanny Burney, a married novelist, in her novels skips any intimate details of childbirth. In *Evelina*, 1778, the fatal birth which occurs in the narrative is quickly over: 'Yet her sufferings were too acute for her tender frame, and the same moment that gave birth to her infant put an end at once to the sorrows and life of its mother.'

Novelists like Mrs Radcliffe and Maria Edgeworth are not to be drawn either into reconstructing scenes of labour and birth in their novels. Charlotte Smith spreads herself a little more on the subject but, after the first few pangs, discretion intervenes to provide a 'fade-out', and no one could guess at what is actually happening when the babies in her novels are being born. Mostly they just 'enter the world' or appear in the room, without any mention of effort. For example, in *Emmeline, or the Orphan of the Castle*, 1789: 'Lady Adeline had, till then, wished to die. She saw her child—and wished to live. The physical people who attended her gave hope that she might.'

These are out-and-out revelations compared with the veiled hints about childbirth which is all the militant modesty of the middle and late nineteenth-century women allows. By some of them the words 'birth' and 'born' are felt to be too coarse, and elaborate euphemisms are manufactured in order to by-pass them and still get across to the reader that a child has been born to a woman. The novelists were on their guard to ensure that no charge of immodesty could be made against them. Charlotte Brontë, writing to Harriet Martineau, begged that she would tell her 'if she considered that any want of womanly delicacy or propriety was betrayed in *Jane Eyre*'.

Miss Martineau, applying the current standards of delicacy and propriety, would certainly have judged any realistic child-birth descriptions as unwomanly and coarse if they had been introduced into a novel. Charlotte, Emily and Anne Brontë all omit childbirth scenes from their novels, although plenty of births take place within the action of them. (Perhaps if Charlotte had not died in early pregnancy she, who had already been judged guilty of immodesty in her writing by many people, including Miss Martineau, would have succumbed to the temptation and written an uninhibited account of pregnancy and labour.) As it was, the sisters, who did not shirk from tackling descriptions of sadistic cruelty, madness and drunkenness, omit childbirth descriptions.

In *Jane Eyre*, 1848, Charlotte Brontë misses out any account of Jane's pregnancy and labour; the child appears in the text when he is put into his father's arms: 'When his first born was put into his arms, he could see that the boy had inherited his own eyes, as they once were, large, brilliant and black.'

Emily Brontë plainly chronicles the births which introduce the second generation into her novel *Wuthering Heights*, 1848. She does not stretch after delicacy to the extent of circumventing the words 'birth' and 'born'; nor does she describe. The births are set down as having taken place without comment: 'On the morning of a fine June day my first bonny nursling and last of the ancient Earnshaw stock was born.'

And further on in the novel: 'About twelve o'clock that night was born the Catherine you saw at Wuthering Heights, a puny seven months' child, and two hours after the mother died having never recovered sufficient consciousness to miss Heathcliff or know Edgar.'

And finally she simply records the birth of Linton: 'I believe her new abode was in the South near London, there she had a son born, a few months subsequent to her escape.'

Anne Brontë, whose work is more conventional than that of her sisters, keeps even more in line with the spirit of the age in her evasion of any words which might possibly evoke a physical image in the reader's mind. One of the most approved and popular ways of referring to childbirth seems to have been to write of it as though it were solely a spiritual experience, a disembodied, religious happening. In Anne Brontë's novel *The*

Tenant of Wildfell Hall, 1848, the mother (who is beginning to feel that she has made an unwise marriage) writes in her diary: 'My bliss is sobered but not destroyed, my hopes diminished but not departed; my fears increased but not confirmed: and, thank Heaven, I am a mother too. God has sent me a soul to educate for Heaven and given me a new and calmer bliss and stronger hopes to comfort me.'

This delicacy is matched by another sample Victorian novelist, Mrs Craik. In her novel *John Halifax, Gentleman*, 1856, the births which occur during this story of family life are recorded in several ways, the most remarkable being the following: 'Thus time went on placidly enough, the father and mother changed into grandfather and grandmother and little Maud into Auntie Maud.'

Mrs Gaskell too, herself a mother of several children, and an author in all of whose eminently domestic novels children are born, includes no details of any confinements. A screen of feminine discretion and propriety is put round all the beds of women in labour. Her nearest approach to a realistic account of what labour is like occurs in *Mary Barton*, 1847. In this book Mrs Gaskell steeled herself to be accurate. Impassioned by the misery of the industrial poor in Manchester, she was determined to show what their life was like in the slum streets. This indignation swept away some of her scruples, and a fatal birth is described with a certain amount of realism—not very much. Mrs Gaskell does not depart far from the feminine tradition. She is a strict censor. No close-ups are allowed; cries are heard, but no sights shown that might suggest what is happening to cause them:

'My missus is in labour, and, for the love of God step in while I run for the doctor, for she's fearful bad.'

While the woman hastily dressed herself, leaving the window still open, she heard cries of agony which resounded in the little court in the stillness of the night . . .

The cries grew worse. The doctor was a long time in hearing the repeated rings at his night bell, and still longer in understanding who it was who made this sudden call upon his services; and then he begged Barton just to wait while he dressed himself in order that no time might be lost in finding the court and the house . . .

'Is she so very bad?' asked he.

'Worse, much worser than I ever saw her before,' replied John.

No, she was not, she was at peace. The cries were still forever . . . The doctor stumbled upstairs by the fire light and met the awestruck look of the neighbour which told him the state of things. The room was still, as he, with his habitual tiptoe step approached the poor, frail body that nothing now could disturb.

This is Mrs Gaskell's most straightforward reference to childbirth. In her other novels she vies with the most prudent women in her evasions of any expression which might be physically suggestive. New babies are revealed, blandly, in their mothers' beds without explanation as to how they got there.

For example, in *Sylvia's Lovers*, 1863: 'But by and by the time came when she was a prisoner in her house: a prisoner in her room, lying in bed with a little baby by her side—her child, Philip's child.'

Finally in *Cranford*, 1891, Mrs Gaskell portrays a community of spinsters of whom Miss Matty is the most childlike. Her married maid, Martha, becomes pregnant; Miss Matty fails to recognize the symptoms, and the appearance of the child astonishes and surprises her almost as much as the reader who has not been prepared either for the arrival of a child. It appears in the text for the first time, chastely wrapped in flannel:

Martha told me she was expecting her confinement very soon—in a week or two and she did not think that Miss Matty was aware of it. . . . One morning within a week after I had arrived I went to call on Miss Matty with a little bundle of flannel in my arms. She was very much awe-struck when I showed her what it was and asked for her spectacles off her dressing table, and looked at it curiously, with a sort of tender wonder at its small perfection of parts.

The omissions by Mrs Gaskell, Mrs Craik, the Brontës and others are contrived with some reticence. In the twentieth century Virginia Woolf, who appears to have a distaste for the physical side of childbirth, contrives her omission blatantly. In her book *Orlando*, 1928, she deliberately wrenches the chapter in which Orlando gives birth, out of its logical course by an ostentatiously artificial break in the narrative in order 'to mitigate, to veil, to cover, to conceal, to shroud' the physical manifestation of childbirth. This is how she manages to make the omission:

Suddenly she [that is Orlando] started—and here we could wish that as on a former occasion Purity, Chastity and Modesty would push the door ajar and provide, at least, a breathing space, in which we could think how to wrap up what has to be told delicately as a biographer should. . . . Is nothing then to happen this pale March morning to mitigate, to veil, to cover, to conceal, to shroud this undesirable event whatever it might be? For after giving a violent start . . . but Heaven be praised at this very moment there struck up one of those frail, reedy, fluty, jerky old-fashioned barrel organs which are still sometimes played by Italian organ grinders in back streets. Let us accept the invitation, humble though it is, as if it were some music of the spheres, and allow it with all its gasps and groans, to fill up this page with sound until the moment comes which it is impossible to deny is coming, which the footman has seen coming and the maid servant; and the reader will have seen too: for Orlando herself is clearly unable to ignore it any longer— let the barrel organ sound and transport us on thought . . .

> . . . here the barrel organ stops playing abruptly. 'It's a very fine boy, M'Lady,' said Mrs Bunting, the midwife, putting her first born into Orlando's arms. In other words Orlando was safely delivered of a son on Thursday, March the 20th at three o'clock in the morning.

In her book *Flush*, 1933, as well as in *Orlando*, Mrs Woolf evinces the same distaste for the physical process of childbirth. The hero of the tale is a dog, Flush, the pet of Elizabeth Barrett Browning. His sufferings during the 'awful event' and his 'deep disgust' at the sight of the newly born child are described with what reads like partisan sympathy:

> People were trampling up and down stairs running and calling in low whispers and muted unfamiliar voices. They were moving upstairs in the bedroom. He crept further and further under the shadow of the sofa. He knew in every fibre of his body that some change was taking place—some awful event was happening . . .
>
> At last Wilson, looking very flushed and untidy, but triumphant, took him in her arms and carried him upstairs. They entered the bedroom. There was a bleating in the shadowed bedroom—something waved on the pillow. It was a live animal. Independently of them all, without the street door being opened, out of herself in the room alone, Mrs Browning had become two people. The horrid thing waved and mewed at her side. Torn with rage and jealousy and some deep disgust that he could not hide, Flush struggled himself free and rushed downstairs.

Anyone with a 'deep disgust' at the sight of a new baby waving and mewing at the side of its mother, and with a distaste for childbirth in general, would do well to steer clear of Mrs

Doris Lessing's *A Proper Marriage*, published 1954, which has in it a documentary-type account of childbirth. It is not recommended for curious schoolgirls, the romantically minded or for those who like their literature to be escapist.

Mrs Lessing's description shows the extent of her break-away from the traditional silence of women. The physical events of pregnancy, labour and the post-natal period are unexpurgated and unromanticized. More than any other account read, this one displays the width of the advantage that a woman has over a man when writing of childbirth.

In the first part of Mrs Lessing's novel Martha's pregnancy is detailed month by month. The following passage occurs at the end of the nine months, and begins with the realization by the heroine, Martha, that at last her labour is starting:

> She was sitting on the floor when there was a small stabbing pain in her vitals. She frowned with concentration; then told herself she was sick and tired of imagining that every twinge was the herald of the end. She was about to get undressed when she felt another. There was no doubt it was of a completely different quality than all the other stabs and twinges. She prowled continuously about the room admonishing the child to keep still, so that she might listen better to the activities of her muscles. The child was seething and striving like a wrestler. It was stilled momentarily on a third stab of pain. Martha was lifted on a wave of excitement: she cried out. Hurray this is it! And like some sort of savage creature proceeded to dance in heavy lopsided triumph round the room. Never had she felt such a soaring elation as this.

Martha arrives at the hospital and is told that she may have a bath:

> Martha flung her cotton smock off with the triumphant thought that she would never have to wear it again. She

heaved herself into the deep, hot water and looked at her stomach. It was now almost square, mottled and streaked, purple, glistening with strain. The baby was as tense as a knot; and Martha's every muscle was braced with the intention of hurrying the process. She lay stiff in the water, her eyes on her watch. Five minutes. Five minutes. Five minutes. The pains came steadily like the strokes of a bell and each time Martha's whole body tensed against them.

After some hours have elapsed, Martha goes into the labour room where she lies down on the hospital couch. The following extracts are taken from the long description of this stage of childbirth:

For some time she lay stiff on the narrow slope of the table and waited. In this position it seemed that the pains were worse. Or rather that she could not command herself as well. She climbed down and walked up and down the deserted room. Now it was every four minutes; and she was doubled up with them, shutting her teeth against a desire to groan, cautiously unfolding herself again. . . . Tight, stiff, cautious, she felt the baby knot and propel itself down; it recoiled and slackened and she with it. The pain had changed. She could mark the point at which, just as it abruptly changed its quality a couple of hours before in the bath, so now it ground into a new gear, as it were. It gripped first her back, then her stomach, then it was as if she and the baby were being wrung out together by a pair of enormous steel hands. But still she kept the small place in her brain alive and watchful. She would not give in. . . . An agony so unbelievable gripped her that her astounded and protesting mind cried out that it was impossible such pain should be. It was a pain so violent that it was no longer a pain but a condition of being. Every particle of flesh shrieked out, while the wave spurted like an electric current from somewhere in her backbone and went through her shock after shock. The wave receded, however, just as she had decided she would disintegrate under it; and then she felt the fist that gripped her slowly loosen. Through the sweat in her eyes she saw that ten seconds had passed; she went limp in a state of perfect painlessness, an exquisite exhaustion, in which the mere idea of pain seemed impossible—it was impossible that it could recur again. And as soon as the slow flush of sensation began, the condition of painlessness seemed as impossible as the pain had seemed only a few moments before. They were two states of being, utterly disconnected, without a bridge and Martha found herself in a condition of anxious but exasperated anger that she could not remember the agony fifteen seconds after it had ended.

. . . She was lying now, almost naked, her great tight-knotted belly sticking up in a purple lump, watching with fascination how it contracted and strained, while she kept alert the determination not to lose control of the process. . . . When the wave of pain had receded and she lay spent, she was grimly flogging her mind to imagine the quality of the pain just gone. Impossible. And when she was writhing in the grip of the giant fist, she was gasping with determination to *imagine* no pain; she could not. With all her determination, she could not.

The agony continues until the second stage of labour is entered upon. In the interim she is examined by doctors and nurses.

('Her plump little hands, tightly sealed in pink rubber, went plunging into Martha's body') and she has had some conversation with a coloured cleaning woman—this is a hospital in South Africa—who attempts to soothe and comfort her. In between this chat and the brightly conducted routine checks of the medical staff Martha is left alone. Now, as the second stage is

reached and the birth becomes imminent, she has the assistance
of doctors, nurses and of anaesthetics:

> Later, Martha heard the bright voice calling, 'Yes, doctor,
> she's ripe!' The room was full of people again. She was
> sucking in chloroform like an addict, and no longer remem-
> bered that she had been determined to see the child born.

(The chloroform obliterates such contacts as that previously
had with 'the pink nurse' who 'lifted her legs, levered them
energetically up and down and said, "That's the stuff, push!"'.)

> When her eyes cleared, she caught a glimpse of Dr Stern
> holding up a naked pallid infant, its dark hair plastered wet
> in streaks to its head, mouthing frustratedly at the air.
> Martha momentarily lost consciousness again and emerged,
> feeling it must be years later, to see Dr Stern in the same
> position, still holding the white baby, which looked rather
> like a forked parsnip and was making strangled grumbling
> gasps. Two nurses were watching him. This humanity
> comforted Martha. She heard someone say, 'A lovely little
> girl, isn't she?' Then the pink nurse bent over her and began
> lifting handfuls of Martha's now slack stomach and squeez-
> ing it like oranges. Martha shrieked, with the intention of
> being heard. 'Oh, drat it,' said the nurse: and the dome of
> white chloroform came down again over Martha's face.

Doris Lessing's account is uninhibited by conventional
modesty; her heroine has an unabashed interest in her body, she
tries to be objective, to observe the physical process of labour
with detachment. Another contemporary heroine with a simi-
larly self-conscious, intellectual approach to her own labour is
Christine, in Pamela Hansford Johnson's novel *An Impossible
Marriage*, 1954. She too tries to maintain a rational control over
her emotions and her body. She is careful to ring the bell for the
nurse, during her labour, only when it is 'reasonable', that is
when she has timed several pains and judged their acceleration.

Like Mrs Lessing's account this one is detailed, and extracts from it are sufficient to convey the atmosphere and tone. Again the account begins in the mother's home with the realization that labour is commencing. The heroine is prepared; she has been all set for the experience for months, and when the pains begin she is ready with her watch:

> It was the middle of the night, warm in bed, cold without, frost ticklish as snuff in the room. My watch had phosphorescent hands. I had timed the intervals: twenty minutes —then fifteen—now ten. Not indigestion . . .
>
> 'How do you feel?'
>
> 'I am quite all right,' I said, feeling set apart, calm, enthroned upon the edge of this adventure. . . . We did not talk much.
>
> 'There it goes again.'
>
> 'There what goes?' said Ned, jumping.
>
> 'The pain.'
>
> 'Oh, God!'
>
> 'It's nothing, hardly anything yet.' I relished the thought of pain to come. It would be exciting.

Like Martha, Christine's next move is to go to the hospital:

> I was examined by the doctor; a little fat nurse came to carry out the humiliating preparations for childbirth. . . .
>
> I think I must have slept for a little while. At last I grew aware (having consulted my watch) that I could reasonably ring the bell again. 'It's every four minutes,' I said.
>
> It was better now I had something to occupy me, something in which I could participate. They let me walk about the room. Between the pains I was perfectly calm indeed for three and a half minutes out of the four, pain was unthinkable. I did not know how anyone could possibly have felt it. But in a while I knew the first touch of panic: for the pain I was now experiencing was not easy to bear and I felt,

indeed, that if it got any worse I should be hard put to endure it.

The nurse who had brought me the magazine studied my face thoughtfully. 'I think we'd better get you along to the labour ward.'

They put me on a trolley and I set out on a strange, dizzying, half-hilarious progress (Macheath to the gallows, I thought) down corridors of light and dark green into a room all white and silver.

'That's the girl,' one of the nurses called to me. She had the jolly, rather weary smile of somebody playing a practical joke.

'One, two and oops we go! Doctor will be here in a minute.'

When he came the Irish nurse told him I was having good pains. I thought it a strange adjective.

After that there was hustle and attentiveness; they touched me where I dreaded to be touched, rallied me, applauded me, told me I was doing well. I thought: Tomorrow must come. Before I know where I am it will be over and I shall say to myself, 'Why, it happened the day before yesterday.' Time has to pass.

I found myself panting, a harsh and ugly noise.

'Degrading,' I managed to say. I heard the doctor laugh. He told me to go on panting: that it was good for me.

'Like a steam engine,' I said, proud that my voice sounded so normal. Then I was engulfed by an agony so extreme to my experience that it felt like some preposterous insult.

'That's right, that's right,' said the doctor. 'You're doing fine.'

In front of my eyes was the lightning-edged scarlet of pain, which is like the colour that lodges under the lids when one tries to sleep in the sun. I did not think of the child, only of myself, only of being brave or not brave. I had a fear of being torn in two. 'But don't worry,' said the cold critic, still present within me and unassailable, 'nobody ever is torn in two.'

'I think', said the doctor, 'that we shall now put you to sleep.'

Another man was standing at my bed. I could see the edge of his white coat.

'Thank you,' I said, as if I had been offered theatre tickets, 'that will be nice,' I added in a gabble, 'just wait until this pain passes——'

'We'll make it pass. You've been very good. Now you shall go to sleep.'

The beautiful anaesthetic was like the fall of velvet over the photographer's camera. I was the camera under the velvet, observing the dark behind me. I saw a green mountain and a river with a water snake of blue glass, swimming with kingly grace towards me. Then, almost, at once,

'Well, there you are, you can wake up: you've got a nice little boy.'

'Have I?' I said. 'Oh, good.'

I saw him held up above the basin, a struggling puppet of vermilion satin, all mouth; his roars split the room. He was wrapped in a blanket and given to me, his small face tight and sulky as if he'd been turned out of heaven during a party.

Well, I thought, well.

I kissed him: he did not seem to belong to me. I touched his little hand and loved him, whoever he belonged to. Then I felt I could kiss the doctor, the anaesthetist, the midwife-nurse. I was full of triumph.

'Thank you,' I said, 'thank you very much, doctor, nurse.' I was glad I was in a fit state to be courteous. I was proud of such courtesy.

... Then it was night again, or perhaps evening. I had had something to eat. I had powdered my face, combed my hair. My body felt strangely soft and flat and light.

Christine is interested in her own labour. She is prepared for childbirth: 'Everything was packed, a list of necessities had reached me months ago.'

She is ready for the hospital, ready for the sequence of pains; she is even armed beforehand with the statistics of the maternal mortality rate. When after the birth the husband confesses how frightened he has been that she might have died while having the baby, Christine replies:

'Of course I wasn't going to die!' I quoted the maternal mortality rate. He damned it.
'It's very low,' I said.

These descriptions by Doris Lessing and Pamela Hansford Johnson of the agonies of childbirth are enough to make the gorge rise of any stalwart exponent of Natural Childbirth. Miss Rebecca West, however, on the evidence of her theory advanced in her novel *The Judge*, published in 1916, would approve wholeheartedly of all this pain—'every particle of flesh shrieked out'—of the 'harsh and ugly' panting and the heightening intensity of pain. This is how childbirth should be; a painless parturition, where the contractions do not hurt, is the one to be regarded with suspicion and terror. A painless birth is unnatural. If, says Miss West in her novel, there is no pain there is something not just lacking in the birth, but something positively wrong. A child who is born in this way will be an object not of joy but of horror to its mother. The concept of pain as an heroic necessary element in childbirth, which brings its own rewards, is first presented in the course of her novel during a conversation between the heroine and her mother-in-law:

'Does having a baby hurt very much?' She did not feel at all disturbed when Marion answered 'Yes', though that was the word she had been dreading, for the speech she added, 'If the child is going to be worth while it always hurts, but one does not care', seemed to be one of those sombre and heartening things like King Lear.

The two births which are subsequently recorded in *The Judge* illustrate the theory. The first child, Richard, who is born to the heroine, is one who was conceived in love. A long and painful labour results in the birth of a strong and beautiful child whom the mother loves. The second child, whose painless labour is described in the following extract, has as its father a man whom the mother found repulsive; his conception is a revolting memory for her. She had hoped, despite this background, that she might be able to feel affection for the child, but when the 'unnatural' birth takes place, she feels that this child, born without her enduring any suffering, can only be antipathetic to her:

She knew she would have no passion for it as she had for Richard, but she foresaw herself being consciously and slantingly tender over it, like a primitive Madonna over the Holy Child. There was, of course, no such solution to the problem. It became plain that there was not going to be in that hour when she knew the horror of a painless parturition. She had not been at all shocked by the violence she had endured at Richard's birth. It had seemed magnificently consistent with the rest of nature, and she had been comforted as she lay moaning by a persistent vision of a harrow turning up rich earth. But contemplating herself as she performed this act of childbirth without a pang was like looking into eyes which are open but have no sight and realising that here is blindness or listening to one who earnestly speaks words which have no meaning and realising that here is madness.

She was going through a process that should have produced life: but because of the lack of some essence which works through pain, but nevertheless is to the breeding womb what sight is to the eye or sanity to the brain, it was producing something that was not so much at variance with life as death. The old women at her bedside chuckled and rubbed their hands because she was having such an easy time but that was because they were old and had forgotten. If a young woman had been there she would have stood at the other side of the room between the windows as far away from the bed as she could, and her lips would have pursed, as if she felt the presence of uncleanness. So were her own when they showed her the pale child. She had indeed done an unclean and unnatural thing when she brought forth a child that lived yet was unloved; who was born of a mother that survived and looked at it, and who yet had no mother since she felt no emotion towards it but a deep shiver of her blood away from it: who aroused no interest in the whole universe save her own abhorrence; who was, as was inevitable, in one so begotten and born, intrinsically disgusting in substance.

In *The Judge* the relationship of the mother to her son is set on its failure course from this beginning of a painless labour. In *The Lost Traveller* by Antonia White, 1950, there is a mother-daughter relationship which is, in a less drastic way, also a failure; in one scene the mother also traces back their relationship to its commencement, Clara's birth. This birth had been prolonged and agonizing, the mother attempts to capitalize her sufferings by recalling them in order to make a futile bid for her daughter's affections; the sufferings in this instance prove as alienating for the child as the painlessness in *The Judge* was for the mother.

'You're so young,' sighed her mother, 'I suppose I ought to be glad you can't even imagine it. I shall never forget what I suffered when you were born. I was so ill they daren't give me chloroform even at the end. And, of course, the first is nearly always the worst. You might think of that sometimes, the agony I went through when you are inclined to look down on me for not being clever. You know how Daddy loves you. But he's never had to prove his love. A mother has to go down to the gates of hell for her child.'

To 'go down to the gates of hell' is not an encouraging way of referring to childbirth when talking to a young girl; Clara is no better off, as far as gaining precise information, than Rosamund Dobson in Mrs Taylor's novel or the Radlett girls in *The Pursuit of Love*. Misconceptions about childbirth are mainly passed around in conversations between schoolgirls and 'old wives', but some are supplied by novels along with other fascinating oddities to do with birth—cauls and birthmarks, phantom pregnancies, baptism of babies in the uterus and other remarkable topics. The novelists bring to light many aspects of the unconscious life of a child-bearing woman. Not only are her weird dreams, the superstitions and portents in which she believes, her secret desires and fears mentioned in English novels, but also the unconscious life of the child itself is written of during its development in the womb through to the final, traumatic act of birth, when it emerges as a separate human being from its mother's womb to start its independent existence.

CHAPTER SIX

SUPERSTITIONS, BIRTHMARKS, PREGNANCY DREAMS AND OTHER ODDITIES

THE talk in the relaxed early evening atmosphere was of monstrous births, of women who had some litters of rabbits or puppies, the superstitions of the very ignorant.

Freakish births like these from Walter Allen's *All in a Lifetime*, 1959, and other oddities connected with childbirth, have a fascination for some novelists as well as for gossiping workers. James Joyce makes an erudite list in *Ulysses*, 1922, of abnormalities and minor deformities to be found in newly born babies: 'The abnormalities of hare-lip, breast-mole, supernumerary digits, negro and inkle, strawberry marks and port-wine stain. . . .'

Dickens also shows an interest in childbirth abnormalities and in childbirth superstitions. In *David Copperfield*, 1849–50, David notes that he was born wearing a 'caul' (a veil of skin which occasionally covers the head of a new-born child) and that, as this was valued as a good luck charm, it was advertised for sale for fifteen guineas in the newspaper. In *Barnaby Rudge*, 1840–1, Barnaby is born with a symbolic birthmark—a blood-stain. During Barnaby's stay in his mother's womb his family is blighted by misfortunes, his father is violently murdered on the very day he is born; and when the unfortunate, simple-minded Barnaby arrives it is noted that because of all this he 'bore on his wrist what seemed to be a smear of blood but half-washed out'.

Scott in *Redgauntlet*, 1824, gives the same reason for a reddish, speckled birthmark:

'See, brother,' she said, pulling her glove off, 'these five blood-specks on my arm are a mark by which mysterious nature has impressed on an unborn infant a record of its father's violent death and its mother's miseries.'

The smear on the wrist and the blood-specks on the arm are minor defects which result from intra-uterine disturbances; more general and long-lasting effects on children, as a result of their mothers' activities during pregnancy, may occur according to other novelists. An extreme example of the dangers of pregnancy for the unborn child is in George Monk's *Bravo of Venice*, 1805, in which a woman expresses her loathing of a villainous-looking man, by remarking:

'If one could look at him without disgust,' murmured Cynthia, 'if he had but the appearance of something human. Satan must certainly have appeared to his mother, while she was big with him and thence came her child into the world with such a frightful countenance.'

If an encounter with the devil by a pregnant woman can produce a hideous appearance in her child when a grown man, such visitations should be carefully avoided: this is a negative resolution to prevent a child from being ugly.

In *Work Suspended*, 1941, by Evelyn Waugh a positive strategy is mentioned whereby a mother hoped to ensure that her child would be beautiful. Lucy says of her mother's pregnancy:

'D' you know before I was born, so Aunt Maureen says, my mother used to sit in front of a Flaxman bas-relief so as to give me ideal beauty.'

Of course it cannot be known until the baby is born if intra-uterine exposure to Art has been effective, and, luckily too, if the

Devil has appeared, his influence on the child's looks cannot be seen until after the birth, but some fictional pregnant women have dreams which have a clairvoyant quality; the mother has the chance to see into her child's future and find out what he is like and what he will do when grown up. (The reader has the added bonus of the rest of the novel, where the heroes' careers are a reflection of the pregnancy dreams' forecast.) One of these clairvoyant dreams occurs in *Roderick Random* by Smollett, 1748. Roderick's mother has the following amazing dream:

> She dreamed she was delivered of a tennis ball which the devil (who to her great surprise, acted the part of a midwife) struck so forcibly with a racket, that it disappeared in an instant; and she was for some time inconsolable for the loss of her offspring; when all of a sudden she beheld it return with equal violence and enter the earth beneath her feet whence it immediately sprung up a goodly tree covered with blossoms, the scent of which operated so strongly upon her nerves that she awoke.

Roderick's parents, understandably, are intrigued and perplexed by the dream and go to a 'wise man' for an interpretation. The 'wise man' is obviously an eighteenth-century forerunner of today's psychiatrist: he is referred to as 'this attentive sage', and after listening well he gives his professional interpretation of the symbolic images only 'after some deliberation'.

Roderick's parents are satisfied with the outcome of their session with him, during which he 'assured my parents that their first born would be a great traveller; that he would undergo many dangers and difficulties and would at last return to his native land where he would flourish in happiness and reputation'.

A satisfyingly optimistic prediction which in the course of the novel is proved to have been correct.

In *Jonathan Wild* by Fielding, 1743, Mrs Wild, like Mrs Random, has a dream while pregnant with the hero of the novel.

Her straightforward, erotic dream is interpreted with mock-seriousness by the author in a comparison between her experience and those of parents in classical stories whose pregnancy dreams preceded the birth of an heroic figure:

> Astaynges, who was the grandfather of Cyrus, dreamed that his daughter was brought to bed of a vine whose branches overspread all Asia: and Hecuba, while big with Paris, dreamed that she was delivered of a fire brand that set all Troy in flames, so did the mother of our Great Man while she was with child with him, dream that she was enjoyed in the night by the gods Mercury and Priapus.

Before the Cavalier's birth in Defoe's *Memoirs of a Cavalier*, 1720, his mother has 'several strange dreams' which, unlike Mrs Wild's, are sufficiently pure to be written down in her prayer book. Two of these, which the Cavalier quotes with the comment, 'if there be anything in dreams', can be interpreted as omens of his future life as a soldier abroad:

> My mother, who was mighty observant that way, took minutes, which I have seen in the leaf of her prayer book, of several strange dreams she had while she was with child of her second son, which was myself. Once she noted that she dreamed she was carried away by a regiment of horse and delivered in the fields of a son, that as soon as it was born, had two wings come out of its back and in half an hour's time, flew away from her: and the very evening I was born she dreamed she was brought to bed of a son and that all the while she was in labour a man stood under her window beating on a kettle drum which very much discomposed her.

[These images, like the tree-image in *Roderick Random*, are given a very different interpretation by the novelists from the explanations of Jung and Freud, and in Scott's *The Pirate* the discrepancy between the interpretation put on Mrs Yellowby's dream of giving birth to a plough in the novel, and Freud's of the same image, makes comparison irresistible. Freud in his *Interpretation of Dreams* comments on a young man's dream of ploughing that he had in his imagination taken advantage of 'an intra-uterine opportunity of watching his parents copulating'; in the novel the explanation of the plough is that it is a sign that the child should be a minister of religion.]

Unfortunately this interpretation provokes a spirited argument amongst the gossips discussing the dream with Mrs Yellowby as to what sort of minister the child should be, whether attached to 'presbytery' or 'episcopacy'. The following extract from *The Pirate* gives the dream and the interpretation, which causes such 'a commotion' that the child is born prematurely and the mother is very ill, though she has enough strength to make her husband promise that the child born after the dream will be educated for the ministry:

Mrs Yellowby had a remarkable dream, as is the usual practice of teeming mothers previous to the birth of an illustrious offspring. She 'was a dreamed', as her husband expressed it, that she was safely delivered of a plough drawn by three yoke of Angusshire oxen, and being a mighty investigator into such portents, she sat down with her gossips to consider what the thing might mean. Honest Jasper, ventured with much hesitation, to intimate his own opinion, that the vision had reference rather to things past than things future and might have been occasioned by his wife's nerves having been a little startled by meeting in the loan of the above house, his own great plough with six oxen, which were the pride of his heart. But the good cummers raised such a hue and cry against this exposition that Jasper was fain to put his fingers in his ears and to run out of the apartment.

'Hear to him,' said an old Whigamore, 'hear to him, wi' his oxen, that as an idol to him even as the calf of

Bethel! Na, na, it's nae plough of the flesh that the bonny lad—bairn—for a lad it sall be, sall e-er striddle between the stilts o'—it's the plough of the spirit—and I trust mysell to see him wag the head o' him in a pu-pit or what's better on a hillside.'

. . . I do not know whether it was impatience to give to the light a being destined to such high and doubtful fates, or whether poor Dame Yellowby was rather frightened at the hurly burly which had just taken place in her presence, but she was taken suddenly ill, and contrary to the formula in such cases used and provided, was soon reported to be 'a good deal worse than expected'. She took the opportunity, having still her wits about her, to extract from her sympathetic husband two promises—first that he would christen the child, whose birth was like to cost her so dear, by a name indicative of the vision with which she had been favoured: and next that he would educate him for the ministry. The canny Yorkshireman thinking she had a good title at present to dictate such matters, subscribed to all she required. A man child was accordingly born under these conditions but the state of the mother did not permit her for many days to enquire how far they had been complied with.'

In *Roderick Random* Smollett writes about another strange phenomenon associated with childbirth, even more extraordinary than these pregnancy dreams recorded by him, Fielding, Defoe and Scott—he describes a 'phantom pregnancy'. He treats this as a joke. Apart from giving Smollett the opportunity for entering the midwife/man-midwife controversy, with a dig at the midwife who stubbornly refuses to admit that she can have made a mistake—the episode has no undertones, it is straightforward comedy without pity. The gusto with which this affliction is turned into a charade by Smollett compels the present-day reader to smile at the false labour of a woman who longs for a

TRISTRAM SHANDY. VOL. II. Ch. 6. P. 12
Corporal Trim reading the Sermon to
Shandy's Father, Dr Slop & Uncle Toby.

From *Tristram Shandy*—how husbands behave

Title-page from the
Little Midwife's Book
—a home confinement

child, and at the persistence, in the face of all evidence, of her hopes and those of her husband, who are 'the standing joke of the parish':

> ... in the middle of the night she [that is Mrs Trunnion, the woman who has the hysterical symptoms of pregnancy] was visited by certain warnings that seemed to bespeak the approach of the critical moment. The commodore got up with great alacrity and called the midwife, who had been several days in the house: the gossips were immediately summoned and the most interesting speculations prevailed, but the symptoms of labour gradually vanished and as the matrons sagely observed this was a false alarm.
>
> Two nights after they received a second invitation and as she was seriously diminished in the waist, everything was supposed to be in a fair way and yet this visitation was not more conclusive than the former, her pains wore off in spite of all her endeavours to encourage them, and the good women took to their respective homes, in expectation of finding the third attack decisive, alluding to the well-known maxim that number three is always fortunate. For once, however, this apothegm failed; and the next call was altogether as ineffectual as the former, and moreover attended with a phenomenon which was equally strange and inexplicable; this was no other than a reduction in the size of Mrs Trunnion as might have been expected after the birth of a fully grown child. Startled at such an unaccountable event, they sat in close divan, and concluding that the case was in all respects unnatural and prodigious, desired that a messenger might be immediately detached for some male practitioner in the art of midwifery.

The suspicions of the onlookers are aroused; they begin to have doubts as to how genuine Mrs Trunnion's claim to be in labour really is, and when 'a surgeon of the neighbourhood who boldly affirmed the patient had never been with child' has spoken up, Mrs Trunnion's delusion is revealed. However, the midwife will still not admit that she has been fooled. She

> still persisted to feed Mrs Trunnion with hopes of a speedy and safe delivery; observing that she had been concerned in many a case of the same nature where a fine child was found, even after all signs of the mother's pregnancy had disappeared. . . .
>
> This experienced proficient in the obstetric art was therefore kept in close attendance for the space of three weeks, during which the patient had several returns of what she pleased herself with believing to be labour pains, till at length she and her husband became the standing joke in the parish, and this infatuated couple could scarcely be prevailed upon to part with their hope even when she appeared as lank as a greyhound and they were furnished with other unquestionable proofs of their having been deceived.

Thackeray in *Henry Esmond*, 1852, also mentions a case of phantom pregnancy: that of a well-born lady who has become a laughing-stock among the nobility because of the persistence of her delusion:

> The court, as I have heard, only laughed the more because the poor lady, who was pretty well passed the age when ladies are accustomed to have children nevertheless determined not to give hope up, and even when she came to live at Castlewood was constantly sending over to Hexton for the doctor and announcing to her friends the arrival of an heir.

The heir never arrives, nor do the children whom Mr Bloom in *Ulysses*, 1922, imagines himself giving birth to: '. . . eight male yellow and white children . . . with valuable metallic faces'.

Speculations and childbirth curiosities abound in *Ulysses*; one of the most interesting is the theologian's opinion, quoted by Joyce, that 'at the end of the second month' in the womb 'a human soul was infused' into the embryo.

On this subject Sterne, in *Tristram Shandy*, includes an irreverent discussion on if it is possible to baptize the soul of a baby doomed to die in the act of birth while it is in the womb: whether it is physically possible, by injection, to administer the water:

> ... that though no part of the child's body should appear that the baptism shall be administered to it, by injection—par le moyen d'une petite canulle—Anglice a 'squirt'. 'Tis very strange that St. Thomas Aquinas who had so good a mechanical head, both for tying and untying the knots of school-divinity, should after so much pains bestowed on this—give up at the point at last as a second 'la chose impossible'. 'Infantes in maternis uteris existentes' (quoth St. Thomas) 'baptizari possunt nullo modo.' O, Thomas! Thomas!

The question of the infant's soul, baptizable or not in the womb, is only one of those mentioned by Joyce in *Ulysees*. He speculates on life in the womb and on what it feels like for the baby when it is born, describing vividly the suffocating terror of infants trying to get out of the womb. When Mr Bloom, who is looking at some old books, sees some pictures of embryos, in an edition of Aristotle, he imagines their frantic activity as they try to get out of the womb:

> Aristotle's masterpiece. Crooked, botched print. Plates; infants cuddled in a ball in blood red wombs like livers of slaughtered cows. Lots of them like that at this moment all over the world. All butting with their skulls to get out of it. Child born every minute.

This image of the curled-up foetus exhaustedly trying to escape from the 'blood red' womb is used by Joyce earlier on in *Ulysses*, during Mr Bloom's recollections of a confinement: 'Child's head too big: forceps. Doubled up inside her trying to butt its way out blindly, groping for the way out.'

Unpleasantness and distress for the child are associated by Joyce with the actual parturition, but not with the intra-uterine life which precedes it. In the hospital sequence in *Ulysses* he writes of life in the womb as being delightful: 'Before birth babe bliss had. Within womb won he worship.'

In *The Unspeakable Skipton*, by Pamela Hansford Johnson, 1959, Skipton is not interested in speculations about the blissful existence in the womb, but he does agree with Mr Bloom about the traumatic quality of birth for the children, and relishes the misanthropic idea that children remember their 'bloody entry into the world, the repulsive captivity of the navel cord' and accordingly loathe their parents. It is debatable whether children can remember their births: in Elizabeth Taylor's novel, *A Sleeping Beauty*, 1959, two children have an exchange of opinions on this:

> 'Babies have no memories,' Constance said, 'or they might remember being born and no one remembers that.'
> 'I do,' said Benjy and then looked away from his mother with embarrassment.
> 'What was it like then?' his sister asked sarcastically.
> 'Oh, nothing much,' he mumbled.

Benjy embarrasses himself by talking about his birth. In Emyr Humphreys's *A Man's Estate*, 1955, a man recalls how, as a child, he was forced frequently to feel acute embarrassment and guilt about his birth. In this novel there is a malicious character, a Miss Aster, who enjoys telling the child of how his mother suffered at his birth, and how, after all the pain for which he is held responsible, he was born looking repulsive:

> It was a notoriously difficult birth. Miss Aster was present and her repeated accounts seem to have registered every agonising record in my memory. . . . My mother was very ill and according to Miss Aster, I was 'the horrid sight', that was my role in her story, 'the horrid sight', . . . 'a lump of raw beef' . . . 'couldn't see your eyes' . . .

Mr Humphrey makes the reader feel indignant that the boy should be indoctrinated to feel guilty about his birth: after all he did not ask to be born; it was not his fault that he was conceived—this is his parents' responsibility. However, Samuel Butler, in *Erewhon*, 1872, takes the opposite view, and blames the child itself for its conception and birth. To be born in his imaginary country is 'a felony for which sentence may be executed at any moment after the commission of the offence'.

The fault lies not in the parents' act but in the will of the unborn child and its conduct. It is a deliberate criminal. Butler's thesis is that the children long to be born, and nag relentlessly at the adults until they consent to bear them. The child is guilty, but the women feel guilty also at succumbing to this invasion of their bodies and, ashamed of the whole business, and their reluctant part in it, they hide away for as long as they can:

> The birth of a child is looked upon as a painful subject on which it is kinder not to touch, and the illness of the mother is carefully concealed until the necessity for signing the birth formula . . . renders further secrecy impossible, and for some months before the event the family live in retirement seeing very little company.

The attitude of the inhabitants of *Erewhon* to the birth of their children is ambivalent. The punishment is not enforced by them, and controversy as to how serious a crime it is is inherent in their treatment of the subject. On one issue they are united: 'The only thing of which they were quite sure was that it was the pestering of the unborn which caused them to be brought into the world and that they would not be here if they had left peaceable people alone.'

One 'unborn' at least in an English novel, could prove himself innocent of this charge of pestering peaceful people to give birth to him. In Mary Shelley's *Frankenstein*, published 1817, the monster does not bully his inventor into giving him life. It is a pity that such an innocent should turn into a horror when filled with life, especially as he has such a good start, no 'butting blindly' to escape from a suffocating womb; created externally, he should start off with an advantage, be a well-adjusted, aneurotic creature. The serenity and silence of his creation, as described in *Frankenstein*, make an outstandingly tranquil and happy contrast to those scenes of sheet-clutching hysteria, filled with screams of pain and agony, which are a routine part of so many descriptions of normal births. The peace at the creation is marred only by the agitation of the inventor; he is not quite confident about his technical skill in creating life. The author, however, makes it all too clear in the novel that this unnatural method of gestation and birth does not pay off, for the only peaceful event in the monster's life and career in *Frankenstein* is his initiation into existence: 'It was on a dreary night of November that I beheld the accomplishment of my toils. With an anxiety that amounted almost to agony, I collected the instruments of life around me, that I might infuse a spark of being into the lifeless thing that lay at my feet.'

In *Brave New World*, published in 1932, by Aldous Huxley, more advanced and intelligent beings are produced by the substitution of scientific techniques for the normal birth process. Huxley's conclusion is the same as Mrs Shelley's in *Frankenstein*: that it is wrong and dangerous to replace the existing mode of birth. In *Brave New World* modern science has made great technical advances on the vague imprecision of the creative work done in *Frankenstein*. The monster's creation has none of the streamlined efficiency of the 'decanting' process used to produce a living human being in the laboratories of *Brave New World*. Untouched by human hand, carefully sterilized, the embryos in their bottles are sped along conveyor belts through their different stages of growth until they achieve independent existence:

Each bottle could be placed on one of the fifteen racks, each rack, though you could not see it, was a conveyor travelling at the rate of thirty-three and a third centimetres an hour.

Two hundred and sixty-seven days at eight metres a day.
Two thousand, one hundred and thirty-six metres in all.
One circuit of the cellar at ground level, one on the first
gallery, half on the second and, on the two hundred and
sixty-seventh morning, daylight in the Decanting Room.
Independent existence—so called!

The elaborate process of 'gestation and birth' is explained to
visitors who are shown round the laboratories. The idea of
normal birth is repugnant and embarrassing to the citizens of the
Brave New World who take a pride in their scientific creation.
Nothing in the laboratories is left to chance. The scientists have
realized that the old 'birth-trauma' might be replaced by the
'trauma of decanting'; this has been taken into consideration by
them and preventive measures put into operation to check the
danger. A lecturer taking a group round the laboratory hinted
'at the gravity of the so-called trauma of decanting, and enu-
merated the precautions taken to minimise, by suitable training
of the bottled embryo, that dangerous shock'.

However, scientific foresight, elaborately sterile conditions and
the rest are not sufficient to compensate for the unnaturalness of the
process; the citizens of the Brave New World who are born in this
way are so standardized and dehumanized as to be as monstrous
and terrifying in their own way as the creature in *Frankenstein*.

Frankenstein and the bottled embryos apart, what happens
during fictional childbirth, whether the woman is squatting, or
sitting in a bearing-down chair, or lying on a bed, is that she is
pushing her child out of her body into the world. Her thoughts
are geared to this physical process. The course of action left
open to the fictional husband is not so well defined. He has to
occupy his mind and body to the best of his ability during the
critical hours which are turning him from a husband into a
father. He must find out himself how he can best make use of
this vacuum in time—for when it has elapsed and his child is
born he knows that he will never be the same again.

CHAPTER SEVEN

HOW HUSBANDS BEHAVE

So THE hours of labour have to be got through somehow by the husbands as well as their wives. The women, at least, have something positive to do; their bodies, the doctors and midwives are directing all their conduct. For the husband there are no definite rules of behaviour. It is an uncharted time for him; no wonder then, at the end of it when the baby is born, that he often breaks out and behaves extraordinarily. Not all of the twenty fictional fathers collected here act in a flamboyant fashion during and after the births of their children. The phlegmatic disinterest in the response of Morel, the miner, in D. H. Lawrence's novel *Sons and Lovers*, 1913, to the announcement that his third child has been born is hardly exuberant: yet there is something rather startling in his lack of pretence of any immediate concern for his wife and baby. Coming home from the pit, for his dinner, he is greeted by his next door neighbour with the news.

'Well,' she said, 'she's about as bad as she can be. It's a boy child.'

The miner grunted, put his empty snap bag and his tin bottle on the dresser, went back to the scullery and hung up his coat, and then came back and dropped into his chair.

'Han yer got a drink?' he asked.

This calm is not shared by some of the other husbands. The whole business unnerved Mr Harris, in Dickens's *Martin Chuzzlewit*, 1843–4, so much that, realizing he was 'so dreadful timid', as soon as his wife started her pains 'he went and stopped

his ears in an empty dog kennel and never took his hands away
or came out until he was shown the baby'.

(No wonder, feeling as he did, that 'he said of his Ninth that
it was one too many if not two'.)

The majority of the husbands in this representational group
from English fiction find themselves seriously emotionally
involved in their wives' labour. The bravest of them actually
stay in their wives' bedrooms in order to encourage their efforts,
the more nervous suffer in sympathy at a distance. The husbands
in the twentieth-century novels are especially sensitive; they tend
to associate themselves closely with their wives' pain, and some
of them feel both angry at the sufferings involved in childbirth,
and guilty. Angry because of the very existence of the pain,
because of the clumsiness of Nature in devising this mode of
entry of life into the world. The primitive incompetence of the
process of birth enrages them ('the process is behind the times').
Their guilt stems, in some cases, from the remembrance of the
part they played in the conceiving of the child. They are responsible for this pain; it arose from their pleasure so, in one
case, the screams of his wife in labour remind the husband that
'he is the cause of this outrageous suffering, not the innocent
child'.

The husbands from the eighteenth- and nineteenth-century
novels are not troubled by this guilt. What they feel mostly
during childbirth is not anger or guilt but fear. For them childbirth results all too often in the death of their wives. Yet sometimes the fear is not of the likelihood of losing their wives but the
less noble one of the expense involved in death and birth. As one
remarks to himself, 'The price of a funeral as well as a birth', or
as another muses grimly, 'Children are expensive'.

This down-to-earth reasoning is matched by the occupations
with which these eighteenth- and nineteenth-century husbands
amuse themselves while their wives are actually giving birth.
Where the guilt-ridden twentieth-century husband paces up and
down in a hospital corridor or, shaken by his powerlessness to

help, and, unable to relax, hovers nervously by the telephone, his matter-of-fact forbears take life easy during the confinement. The unfortunate modern husband is to be discovered doing such things as lying outside the bedroom door in tears, and walking distractedly through the empty night streets. If he is allowed into the bedroom he appears to become even more stricken and remorseful, and may even be permanently changed by the experience. He is a lonely, unhappy figure, unlike the earlier Englishman, who, although often worried about the safety of his wife, or about the increase in his financial liabilities as a result of the birth, has plenty to distract him and make him cheerful during his wife's labour.

It appears from Fielding's novel *Amelia*, published 1756, that it was common practice for a husband to hold a confinement party while his wife was in labour. These parties seem to have been riotously gay with plenty of drinking—a confinement was a splendid excuse for a really jolly party. It is with amazement that Miss Mathew, in *Amelia*, hears that Booth, Amelia's husband, did not get drunk while she was giving birth to his child, but that he actually made his wife some 'caudle'—a spicy, hot wine which was supposed to be of benefit to women during childbirth:

'I thought the best of husbands had looked upon their wives' lying-in as a time of festivity and jollity. What, did you not even get drunk in the time of your wife's delivery? Tell me honestly how you employed yourself at this time?'

'Why then, honestly,' replied he, 'and in defiance of your laughter, I lay behind her bolster and supported her in my arms; and upon my soul I believe I felt more pain in my body than she underwent in her body. And now answer me honestly, do you really think it is a proper time for mirth when the creature one loves to distraction is undergoing the most racking torments as well as the most imminent dangers?'

Cancelling the confinement party and staying with one's wife during her labour was evidently in those days an eccentric way of behaving, inviting ridicule. Scott in *Guy Mannering*, 1815, gives a portrait of a more conventional husband than Booth, and describes how he behaved during his wife's confinement. The Laird in *Guy Mannering* has no inhibitions about staying out of his wife's room and not 'making her caudle'. He sits comfortably chatting to a guest and listens with enjoyment to songs and gossip. He does not feel so detached as to go to bed: 'I cannot weel sleep until I hear she's gotten over with it.' And he has 'the anxious feelings of a father in such a predicament'; nevertheless there is a pleasantly cosy atmosphere in the downstairs part of the house.

Childbirth, according to Scott's description in *Guy Mannering*, was looked upon as a merry time, and a good excuse for extra food and drink in Scotland too. To celebrate the baby's arrival special festive food and drink were prepared for the husband and his friends. The appropriate drink for a confinement party in Scotland was aptly called 'groaning malt', a powerful ale which was poured ready to be drunk as soon as the news filtered from upstairs that the child had been born. To go with the groaning malt was a large rich cheese-cake, called the 'kenno', which was supposed to be secretly prepared as a surprise treat for the husband, and which was served to the new father and then to his guests and the household and anyone else who happened to be present at the party. There is, at the gathering described in *Guy Mannering*, a prevailing feeling of security and content—an air of assurance that everything is sure to be going well up above. The 'howdie', as the midwife is called, is 'very expeditious', says the Laird complacently, and he only goes into his wife's room when the birth is well over and he has heard 'the joyful annunciation' that the lady 'has presented him with a fine boy'.

The good time which the Laird and other fictional husbands had in those days was made possible through the considerate conduct of the women, and especially of the wives, during labour. There is a toughness displayed by the eighteenth- and early nineteenth-century mothers and their female assistants. They have a strong sense of feminine propriety in their behaviour. They are determined not to fuss or alarm their menfolk during childbirth. Whereas in most of the later nineteenth-century fiction and in modern novels the husbands are portrayed as hearing the most terrifying screams and dreadful moans and gasps, the eighteenth-century fathers are portrayed as being shielded from any of the noisy distress which may accompany childbirth. Their wives do not seem to have exhibitionistic tendencies when they are in labour; they rely on their midwives and other female helpers, who all conspire to hide any of the unpleasant side of childbirth from the expectant father. Everything is tidied up before he is admitted to the bedroom. The modesty and reticence of the women are studied in the attempt to protect the men from any upsetting scenes.

A confinement scene from *The Fortunate Mistress*, by Daniel Defoe, published 1724, gives an example of this sort of cheerful fortitude which was summoned up by a woman of that time, in order to give the father-to-be an easy time during the birth. A mistress, of course, has more incentive than a wife for showing consideration to the father of her child. An ugly scene might be off-putting. The Fortunate Mistress runs no risk of upsetting the Prince, her protector, and earns his gratitude.

The following account which the Fortunate Mistress gives of her confinement provides an exemplary model for a mistress, or a wife, of how to keep a man happy during childbirth:

'When I found that my time was come, it fell out very happily that he [that is the Prince] was in the house and I entreated he would continue a few hours in the house, which he agreed to; they called his highness to come into the room if he pleas'd as I offer'd and desired him, and I sent word I would make as few cries as possible to prevent disturbing him: he came into the room once and call'd to me to be of

good courage: it would soon be over, and then he withdrew
again: and in about half an hour more Amy carried him the
news that I was delivered and had brought him a charming
boy; he gave her ten pistolets for her news, stayed 'till they
had adjusted things about me, and then came into the room
again, cheer'd me and spoke kindly to me, and look'd on the
child; then withdrew; and came back the next day to visit
me.'

Nothing happens in the Prince's presence during this confinement to make him overwrought or anxious. No one expects him
to make any difficult decisions or to help in any way. The
women have seen to it that everything is under control. All the
Prince has to do is reward the midwife with money, and his
mistress with his approval and interest. Like the Laird's wife, she
is not described as giving birth to a son; she has 'brought the
Prince' a 'charming boy'. It is for his benefit and gratification.

Another record of the carefree time afforded to an Englishman in an eighteenth-century novel, during his wife's confinement, is given in *Tristram Shandy* by Laurence Sterne, 1760–8.
Mr Shandy is portrayed as already having enjoyed the nine
months of his wife's pregnancy thoroughly. He has read up on
the subject of childbirth and decided that he likes the idea of his
wife having a Caesarean section best, but will settle for a feet-
first delivery if he cannot have his way about the operation.
During his wife's labour he relishes every detail of the 'racket
overhead' as he sits swapping anecdotes with Uncle Toby.
Their chat is interspersed by ribald discussions with Dr Slop
and the midwife on such topics as where to, and particularly
where not to, grip the foetus with the forceps if the child is a
boy. There is no doubt from Sterne's evidence that a man can
enjoy childbirth positively, provided he has the right mental
attitude to the subject.

Mr Shandy has no desire to play the part of the anxious father
during the confinement. Not so Mr B. in Richardson's novel

Pamela, 1740. Here is an eighteenth-century father-to-be who feels it incumbent on him to show by a display of anxiety, with it seems some relish, that he is a man of great sensibility. During Pamela's confinement he is busy acting out his concern for his wife 'with trembling impatience'. However, his distress is to be taken with a pinch of salt when it is realized that his performance takes place downstairs, well out of earshot of any sound from Pamela's room, and away from any of the mess and horror attendant on the birth of his child. He is not told what is happening until the birth is safely over and the women are quite sure all is well. Only then does one of them come downstairs to reassure and congratulate him:

'A boy, a fine boy, dear Mr B.!' said I. 'A son and heir indeed.'

'But how does my Pamela? Is she safe? Is she like to do well?'

'We hope so,' said I, 'or I had not come down to you, I'll assure you . . .'

'If my Pamela is safe, the boy is welcome indeed! But when may I go up to thank my Jewel?'

Mr B.'s florid anxiety is groundless. Pamela, although she has had 'a sharp time', is not in danger and both she and the child do well. But death and birth happened too often together in those days for many fictional husbands to escape bereavement. Clara Reeve, in her novel *The Two Mentors*, 1783, paints a full-length portrait of a husband who sees his wife die in childbed. The husband, an anonymous nobleman at this stage in the novel, abandons all control during his wife's childbed fever and death. The dying wife behaves throughout with calmness and dignity, the husband with wild hysteria. What is fascinating in this contrast is that none of the other characters in the novel find this at all remarkable. The husband throughout is looked after with tenderness and sympathy. He does not feel obliged to keep a stiff upper lip—it is not expected of him.

What happens is this. A mysterious husband and wife are forced in the emergency of her premature labour and feverish condition to knock at the door of a clergyman's house and ask for assistance. The clergyman and his wife take the couple in and spare no effort to look after both wife and husband equally. The clergyman 'rides as upon life and death' to fetch a doctor to aid the midwife; the husband is too distracted to do anything useful. While the wife is carried upstairs and attended to by the women of the house and the doctor and midwife, he is comforted downstairs by the clergyman and others. After two hours one of the women comes downstairs and reports that the lady is delivered and is alive, and so is the child, but it is uncertain how long the wife will continue so. The husband begs to see his wife but is protectively told that it is better that he does not for the present. He remains below until 'after some hours', when it is realized that the wife is dying and that the husband cannot be shielded any longer. Reluctantly he is allowed into her room, after being kindly cautioned to try to control himself. The following 'mournful scene' takes place when the husband sees his dying wife.

My wife [that is the clergyman's wife] was supporting the dying lady, her arm under her head, and she held my Maria's hand to her lips. Mrs Horton held the child for the mother to take a last look at it. The lady spoke in a low, tremulous voice:

'You will be the mother of my child?'

'I will,' said my wife in low, faltering tones; 'she shall be as dear to me as my own.'

'Thank you, my dear friend, God bless you.'

The husband ran to the bedside: he kneeled by it; he sobbed but could not speak; he took her hand with my wife's in it; she tried to turn that way but could not. She said:

'Farewell, dear love! Take care of yourself; do not

grieve for me; your father, your child! Live long and happy. God bless, bless, keep you.'

She fell into a fit with this exertion. We carried the distracted man out of the room and she expired a few minutes after. The husband was in agonies; he raved till his strength was exhausted and then sank into fainting fits.

Everyone rallies round the fainting man; he is pitied, nursed and finally bled as a measure to help him recover from his grief. The clergyman 'begged the doctor to stay with us to take care of him'; the doctor agrees:

'I will bleed him,' said he; 'I make no doubt he will soon recover; this kind of grief is not fatal; it is the *silent kind* which preys upon the heart!'

He bled the patient, we laid him down in the bed: I left my servants and the neighbour's son to watch with him, with orders to call me if I was wanted.

The servants and the neighbour's son accept the charge of caring for the new father without question, and, when the husband has somewhat recovered, more sympathy and attention are given to him. The clergyman weeps 'with him in silence; he poured forth his acknowledgements for my tender sympathy'.

The husband is spared even having to make the funeral arrangements; the clergyman has a family vault and is willing to 'give our guest a place in it'.

Two features in these scenes from *The Two Mentors* are of especial interest. One is this way the husband has of giving way to his grief in public without causing any surprise or criticism. It is not a private tragedy.

The other striking feature in this account is the indifference of the father to his child, whose presence does not help to mitigate his grief, nor does anyone expect it to do so, least of all the dying mother, as she asks the clergyman's wife to be 'the mother of her child'—a woman who is a complete stranger to her and her

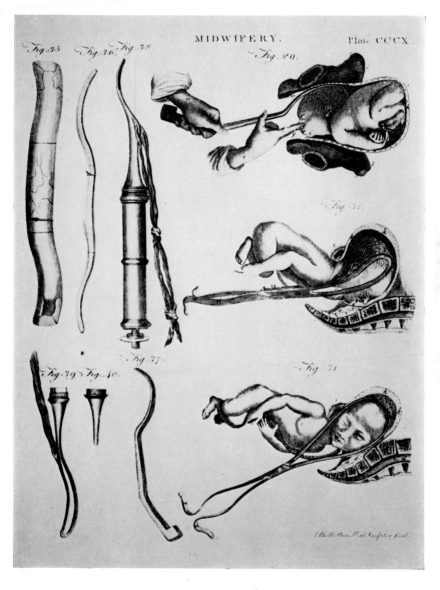

Midwifery instruments and methods of delivering babies with forceps—
late 18th century

New-born child
and Mother—
17th-century French
engraving

husband. The clergyman's wife takes this trust and is accepted by the father, at once, as a substitute parent. She is found 'giving her own breast to the poor orphan child, while the tears rolled down her cheeks in compassion'.

The father feels that his parental responsibility is merely a financial one. With splendid understatement he takes the clergyman on one side and confides:

'I ought to do *something* towards providing for this poor child. I will deposit a sum in your hands for her use and benefit; the interest of it you will accept for her board and necessaries.'

The romantic idea of the child taking its mother's place in his affections does not enter his head and, having fixed up the financial arrangements, he sets off on his travels.

This husband's worst fear of his wife's death is realized. Childbirth arouses other fears in men; as well as death to worry about there is often money to consider. To some fictional husbands comes the fearful thought of how expensive the business of birth is. In *Adeline* by Mrs Opie, published in 1804, there is one of the earliest examples of the fathers whose concern is over the cash expenditure involved in bringing up a child. Here the husband, Berrendale, is a man who loves his wife, after his fashion, but he is not a sentimental man; money means a good deal to him. After the gush of Mr B. and the afflictions of the husband in *The Two Mentors*, there is something both refreshing and funny in the honesty of Berrendale's thoughts when he sees his child for the first time, and in the way in which he consoles himself: 'True he rejoiced in Adeline's safety but he said within himself, "Children are expensive things and we may have a large family", and leaving the bedside as soon as he could, he retired to endeavour to lose in an afternoon's nap, his unpleasant reflections.'

In a novel written towards the end of the nineteenth century a husband appears who has a similar reaction to childbirth. It is the money needed for a child which haunts him. But Bob, the father-to-be, in Gissing's novel *The Nether World*, 1889, is a far more under-privileged member of society than Berrendale. It would be impossible to imagine him taking an afternoon nap to rid himself of the nagging thought of how much an increase in family will cost. For Bob, an impoverished slum dweller, another child is just another mouth to feed. His anxiety over money is so bitter that the child's death causes him relief, not sorrow. In the following stark conversation he hears of the death of his newly-born child:

> 'Is your wife upstairs, Mr Hewett?' Jane asked when he had nodded sullenly in reply to her greeting.
> 'Yes, and somebody else too as could have been dispensed with. There's another mouth to feed.'
> 'No, there ain't,' cried a woman's voice just behind him.
> Jane recognised the speaker, a Mrs Griffin, who lived in the house and was neighbourly to Pennyloaf.
> 'There ain't?' inquired Bob gruffly.
> 'The child's dead.'
> 'Thank goodness for that anyway.'

Besides not saying he is sorry that the baby is dead, Bob does not talk either about his wife's sufferings during childbirth; he does not say or think that her pains are disturbing. He does not feel guilty. In more modern novels there are several husbands who have the leisure and the sensitivity to feel sorrow, guilt and remorse when their children are being born. Childbirth is a dreadful occasion for them: they are appalled by their wives' misery, remembering their part in conceiving the child. Of these husbands, one who feels miserable and ashamed during his wife's labour is the Mummer, created by George Moore in his novel *The Mummer's Wife*, published in 1884.

The Mummer, a down-at-heel actor, is sitting in the next room to the one in which his wife Kate is, so he can hear all her screams. As with Berrendale and Bob, the price of the whole thing weighs on him, but unlike them he goes beyond these fears and worries about the sufferings of his wife, clumsily questioning what it all means and how responsible he is for her pain. These are his first rambling thoughts:

There were a thousand things that would have to be paid for—the baby's clothes, the cradle, the——, he tried to think of what was generally wanted under such circumstances, but the cries in the next room which had gradually swelled into shrieks appalled him, and involuntarily the thought struck him that there might be a funeral to pay for as well as a birth.

The sounds of agony provoke more complicated thoughts; large, vague ideas about God and Birth drift through his fuddled mind:

'Was this life?' he asked himself, 'or death? And by whose order was a human creature tortured thus so cruelly?' But the idea of God did not arrest his attention and his thoughts fixing themselves on the child he asked himself what was this new life to him?

These reflections are interrupted by renewed shrieks coming from the bedroom, from which the following words may 'be distinguished':

'Oh, I never will again! Oh, how I hate him—I could kill him. I'll never love him, never no more.'

These words give the Mummer the shocking idea that it is he who is responsible for this agony:

The cry touched the fat Mummer through all the years of gross sensuality, through the indigestion of his big dinner, and struck by the sense of her words, he shuddered, remembering that he was the cause of this outrageous suffering and not the innocent child.

His shame persists after he goes into the bedroom and is shown the child:

'It's a little girl—kiss it, dear.'
He awkwardly touched with his lips the tiny whining mass of flesh the nurse held forward, feeling without knowing why—ashamed of himself.

The Mummer has to be prompted by his wife's screamed resolution, 'I'll never love him, never no more', before he connects his love-making with her pain in childbirth and before he feels guilty. He is not normally an introspective man. In *Lady Chatterley's Lover*, 1932, D. H. Lawrence describes a more seriously minded husband whose sensitivity makes the Mummer's awkward shame pale by comparison. Mr Bolton is not just an eavesdropper like the Mummer—he stays in his wife's bedroom and is an eye-witness of what he thinks of as the direct result of his love-making. His wife says afterwards that it was a bad mistake [her mother-in-law's] to let him stay in the room. Bolton is horrified by what he sees and hears and can never forget the scene. In his shocked simplification, childbirth means that sexual intercourse can result in dreadful physical sufferings. The pleasure of the sex act is, from then onwards, associated with the pains of childbirth, and as a result he becomes semi-impotent, incapable of making love to his wife without tension and misgiving, because he cannot bear the thought that he might cause a repetition of the suffering which he has seen. Here is how Mrs Bolton tells Lady Chatterley (Connie) about her husband's behaviour during and after the confinement, and of the effect that witnessing the birth had on their subsequent married life:

'The way he sat when my first baby was born, motionless and sort of fatal eyed he looked at me, when it was all over! I had a bad time, but I had to comfort him. "It's all right lad, it's all right!" I said to him. And he gave me a look and a funny sort of smile. He never said anything, but I don't believe he had any right pleasure with me ever after, he'd never let himself go. I used to say to him "Oh let thysen go lad!"—I'd talk broad to him sometimes. And he said nothing. But he wouldn't let himself go or he couldn't. He didn't want me to have any more children. I always blamed his mother for letting him in the room. He'd no right t'ave been there. Men make so much more of things than they should when they start brooding.'

'Did he mind so much?' said Connie in wonder.

'Yes, he sort of couldn't take it for natural all that pain. And it spoilt his pleasure in his bit of married love. I said to him "If I don't care why should you? It's my look out!" But all he'd ever say was "It's not right."'

'Perhaps he was too sensitive,' said Connie.

This seems fair comment by Connie. Bolton is one of the husbands who suffer as they become fathers in the course of some of D. H. Lawrence's novels. His husbands all suffer, but differently. Bolton's fastidious physical shrinking is simple, and his subsequent behaviour logical, if extreme. In *The Rainbow*, 1915, Lawrence analyses the reactions of another tortured husband whose wife is in childbirth. He is more complicated. Brangwen feels alien to his wife during her labour and yet involved in the closest possible way. He has with his wife a semi-mystical union of suffering, so that he participates spiritually in the pain. The union of marriage, the concept of 'two in one flesh', is so real for him that he claims to share the pain. His sufferings are fused with those of his wife. For him the violence of the sex act is analogous to the violence of childbirth. Just as the two were united in the act of love to conceive the child, so the two are equally associated in the birth. The 'life' came from the man into the submissive woman who conceived. Now the life comes out of her body while the man submits, spiritually, to the violence of her birth pains:

On her the blows fell, but the quiver ran through him, to his last fibre. She must be torn asunder for life to come

117

forth, yet still they were one flesh, and still further back the life came out of him to her and still he was the unbroken that has the broken rock in its arms, their flesh was one rock from which the life gushed out, of her who was smitten and rent: from him who quivered and yielded.

Despite this theory of the unity of love-making and birth, he feels alien to his wife when he sees her in labour: he knows that he is separated by the physical spasms which convulse the female body alone.

Brangwen, writes Lawrence, when he sees his wife enduring a contraction 'turned away white to the gills'; and later on, 'when her pains began afresh, tearing her, he turned aside and could not look'.

He comes out of the room. This is an understandable, if outwardly unsympathetic, way of behaving. The pains affect Brangwen spiritually so profoundly and yet he cannot physically communicate this unity of their suffering to his fellow sufferer. It is a human if selfish reaction. *He* could not bear it! It stands in contrast to the mental robustness of Booth in Fielding's *Amelia*, who too claims to feel the same pain, or more, in his own body as his wife does in hers, but who sits behind his wife's pillow and gives her his physical, as well as his moral, reassurance and support.

Lawrence claims that Brangwen is suffering as much as his wife; there is no doubt that he is having a terrible time. This claim is exceeded further on in *The Rainbow* when it is the turn of Will, Brangwen's son-in-law, to be subjected to the strains of childbirth. Instead of 'turning away white to the gills' and leaving his wife alone as Brangwen did, he, with masochistic stoicism, sits out his wife's labour in her bedroom, and has such a frightful time that Lawrence is moved to comment: 'Probably he suffered *more* than she did. He was not shocked or horrified. But he was screwed very tight in the vice of suffering.'

Will's sufferings, unlike poor semi-impotent Mr Bolton, have no long-term effects. They end with the birth, and he is amply compensated for being screwed in the vice of suffering by experiencing, after the birth, a great wave of paternal love. Anna's baby is a girl and she is momentarily disappointed. Will senses this and 'a great blazing passion of resentment and protest sprang up in his heart. In that moment he claimed the child'.

Will's claim of the child, his immediate recognition of its importance to him, has affinities with the strong paternal feeling of another fictional father, Soames Forsyte, the main character in Galsworthy's *The Forsyte Saga* (vol. ii: *In Chancery*, 1920–9) of about the same date. The similarity between the two men's feelings is that both make a passionate identification with their first and, in Soames's case, his only child. But Soames's passion springs from a different source from Will's simple love, which is protective in origin. Soames's love is possessive. The source of his love is his ownership of the child—she is a prized belonging. All during his wife's labour he is thinking of how much he must have a child of his own. The urge to have a child of his own is made particularly striking as it is heightened by the decision he has to make when the doctor tells him that an operation will save his wife's life but will kill the child, and if the operation is not done the danger for both is grave. Either way Annette, his wife, will never have any more children. Soames chooses not to have the operation performed; his decision is partly tempered by his lack of love for his wife, but is made, for the most part, because he wants a child so urgently. Soames would have no sympathy or understanding for the husband in *The Two Mentors*—heart-broken over his wife's death and unconcerned with his daughter; with Soames it is the other way round. He does not care if his wife dies so long as his child lives. This is an extract from Galsworthy's description of Soames during his wife's confinement:

He looked at his watch. In half an hour the doctor would be back. He must decide. If against the operation and she died how face her mother and the doctor afterwards? How face his own conscience? It was his child she was having. If for the operation—then he condemned them both to childlessness. And for what else had he married her but to have a lawful heir?

The news comes that the baby has been born:

He dashed up the four steps in front of him and came suddenly on the doctor in the dim passage. The man was wiping his brow.

'Well,' he said, 'quick.'

'Both living: it's all right, I think.'

Soames stood quite still, covering his eyes.

'I congratulate you,' he heard the doctor say; 'it was touch and go.'

Soames is told that his child is a girl. As has been noted he is violently disappointed until he sees his daughter for the first time. He looks into the cot:

It had dark hair. He touched it with his finger, he wanted to see its eyes. They opened, they were dark—whether blue or brown he could not tell. The eyes winked and stared—they had a sort of sleepy depth in them. And suddenly his heart felt queer, warm as if elated.

'Ma petite fleur,' Annette said softly.

'Fleur,' repeated Soames, 'Fleur, we'll call her that.'

The sense of triumph and renewed possession swelled within him.

'By God, this—this thing was *his*.'

Soames spent the hours during which Fleur was being born in a ghastly state of isolation with nothing to do but make his vital decision and review all the gloomy possibilities of his action. In a later volume of *The Forsyte Saga* (*The White Monkey*) Fleur marries, and in her turn is confined. Michael,

Soames's son-in-law, does not have his problem over whether the doctor should operate or not, but he has plenty of his own gloomy speculations to keep him in a constant state of misery. What does childbirth mean? he asks himself. Why is there this terrible moaning? Michael's puzzled thoughts are a far cry from the unquestioning acceptance of the Laird that the midwife is doing her job well; and the way in which Michael and Soames pass the time is remote from the 'best of husbands' who got drunk in the eighteenth century. In place of their laughter and gossip is the solitary despair of Michael. He is described as rushing up and down stairs, listening at the door of Fleur's bedroom and then dashing downstairs, appalled, eager to get out of earshot; as being sent out to fetch his father-in-law, Soames, and then, as bleakly, spending his nerve-racked vigil in his frigid company. Listening to each moan and cry, and wincing together at every one, Michael and Soames sit in silence, pathetically holding hands to give each other a bit of comfort. No jokes, no wine and food, no cheerful speculations and chat, only the sober unuttered monologue by Michael, unable as he is to communicate his fears and bewilderment to anyone:

'This is how one becomes a father,' he thought. 'This is how I became a son!' That moaning. He could not bear to stay there, and he could not bear to go away. It might be hours yet. He kept repeating to himself: 'One must not worry—must not worry!' How easily said. How meaningless. . . . Why should birth be like this? And the answer was: it isn't in China. To have a creed that nothing mattered—and then run into it like this. Something born at such a cost, must matter, should matter. One must see to that! Speculation ceased in Michael's brain: he stood listening terribly. Nothing. He could not bear it down there and went up again. No sound at first, and then another moan. . . .

There it was again! Back he flew upstairs with his ears covered and his eyes wild.

After the birth of his son has been announced Michael goes into his wife's room. He feels that Fleur, his wife, has been separated from him by the pain (no Lawrentian fusion of suffering has been experienced). The following conversation takes place:

'I mustn't talk,' said Fleur, 'but I want to frightfully; as if I had been dumb for months.'

'Just as I felt,' thought Michael, 'she's been away, away somewhere; utterly away.'

'It was like being held down, Michael. Months of not being yourself.'

Michael said softly:

'Yes, the process is behind the times. Has he got any hair? My mother wants to know.'

Michael's misery during Fleur's confinement is aggravated by his having nothing to do. He is an outsider with no purpose to serve. He has no comfort offered to him. The only personal contact he is offered, apart from sitting mute with Soames, is the chance to listen to his wife's screams. The doctor and midwife take charge; the only course left to him is to brood. Another husband made redundant during his wife's labour is Trafford, the hero of H. G. Wells's *Marriage*, 1912. Trafford is even worse off than Soames or Michael, for he has the bad luck to have an old-fashioned, incompetent doctor to attend at the confinement. He refuses to blunt the wife's pains with any form of anaesthetic, consequently the screams of Marjorie, Trafford's wife, are heard incessantly by Trafford. The labour is prolonged. Throughout it Trafford paces alone, up and down the garden. Apart from the disturbing interruption of being sent off to 'fetch a special sort of needle that the fool of a doctor had forgotten', and having his worse forebodings about the doctor's ability confirmed by a brief discussion with the nurse who describes 'the doctor's methods scornfully', Trafford is left absolutely alone in the company of his own unhappy thoughts.

If anything he stands up to this ordeal less well than Michael, who tried to do a little positive thinking. All Trafford wants to do is murder the doctor—an urge which he realizes would not be of any practical help: 'Was she dying? Were they murdering her? It was incredible this torture could go on. Somehow it must end. Chiefly he wanted to go in and kill the doctor. But it would do no good to kill the doctor.'

Lonely and suffering, Trafford is at last given the news that Marjorie has had a daughter. When he is shown his new child his overwhelming feeling for it is pity for its weakness and for its unattractiveness.

> Presently they brought out a strange wizened little animal, wailing very stoutly, with a face like a very old woman with reddish skin and hair—it had quite a lot of wet blackish hair of an incredible delicacy of texture. It kicked with a stumpy monkey's legs and inturned feet. He pitied it beyond measure, it was so weak and ugly.

Trafford breaks down and cries without restraint when he is finally able to see Marjorie after the birth. When, in Defoe's novel *The Fortunate Mistress*, the Prince saw his mistress, after the birth of their son, she was all tidied up and the visit was a social occasion. Trafford is told to go in to Marjorie when she is lying exhausted 'amidst a litter of surgical precaution'. He re-encounters Marjorie in this ominous muddle for a few minutes before he is sent out to take refuge in the garden again:

> Later for just a little while he was permitted to see Marjorie —Marjorie so spent, so unspeakably weary, and yet so reassuringly vital and living, so full of gentle pride and gentler courage amidst a litter of surgical precaution that the tears came streaming down his face and he sobbed shamelessly as he kissed her. 'Little daughter,' she whispered and smiled—that dear, sweet smile of hers! and closed her eyes and said no more.

Afterwards as he walked up and down the garden, he remembered their former dispute and thought how characteristic it was of Marjorie to have a daughter in spite of all his wishes.

Trafford is not the only father in an early twentieth-century novel to weep while his wife is in labour. Gino, in E. M. Forster's *Where Angels Fear To Tread*, 1905, has a highly emotional reaction to his wife's labour. He does not walk in the garden like Trafford, but lies outside his wife's door. He is not tense with anxiety that his wife might die—just as well because she does; what makes him 'half unconscious' is the intensity of his desire for a child:

> Before the child was born he gave her a kiss and said,
> 'I have prayed all night for a son.'
> Some strangely tender impulse moved her and she said faintly,
> 'You are a boy yourself, Gino.'
> He answered,
> 'Then we shall be brothers.'
> He lay outside the room with his head against the door like a dog. When they came to tell him the glad news they found him half unconscious, and his face was wet with tears.
> As for Lilia, someone said to her:
> 'It's a beautiful boy!'
> But she had died in giving birth to him.

Hospitals do not permit husbands to lie outside their wives' doors during childbirth, and in C. P. Snow's novel, *Homecomings*, 1959, Lewis's wife Margaret goes into hospital to have their child, so he has to find some other place to be in while she is giving birth. He fills in the time from when he takes her to hospital to when he hears that the child is born by going out to dine, and then coming home to bed. This seemingly stodgy way of behaving is deceptive: Lewis, as can be seen from the way he behaves when his friend Charles March, the doctor, telephones him to announce the birth of his son, is another sensitive emotional husband. His emotions are of fear mixed with great joy, and, when he sees the baby, of paternal protectiveness. After the telephone call, during which Lewis has been told that, as it is the middle of the night, he cannot see his wife and child until the morning, and Charles has suggested he should go back to bed, he dresses and goes out to roam around the dark streets:

I dressed and went down into the street where the night air was thundery and close. Just as, when expecting a joy and suddenly dashed with disappointment, one has moments when the joy is still expected, just so, the shadow of fear can survive the opposite shock, the shock of happiness.

It was not until I saw Margaret the next morning, how-ever, that I felt happy. Suddenly the sight of her in bed, her hair as straight as a schoolgirl's, her collar-bone plain where the bed jacket and night gown had fallen away, made the tear glands smart, and I cried out. I said I had not seen her look like that; then when I let her go and gazed at her again I had to ask,

'How are you?'

'What century do you think you're living in?'

She was tired and spoke with the indulgence of not concentrating. She went on,

'I wish I could have another for you.'

I interrupted her, and then she said, inspecting me,

'What do you think you've been doing?'

'Walking about.'

Eliot is shown the child:

I was looking at the eyes unfocussed, rolling and unstable, the hands waving slowly and aimlessly as anemones. I felt utterly alien from this being in her arms: and at the same time I was possessed by the insistence in which there was nothing like tenderness, which was more savage than tender, that he must live and that nothing bad should happen to him.'

Lewis is quite sure that the birth of his son is an event of extraordinary significance in his life. For Rickie too, another fictional husband from the fifties, the central character in Rosamund Lehmann's *The Echoing Grove*, the birth of his daughter is so important that he feels that it can change his entire mental outlook. His reaction to the birth of his third child and first daughter, although confused by the emotional entanglements of his private life, is one of great, reviving, clearly felt joy. This is an event which can alter his life, which alone can give him hope and a purpose for continuing to live.

In the novel Rickie has been unfaithful to his wife Madeleine by having a love-affair with his sister-in-law Dinah. The child whose birth he awaits, as he sits alone downstairs, was conceived during a pseudo-reconciliation between himself and his wife. Because of the circumstances in which the child was conceived, Rickie has been fearful during the pregnancy that it would be some 'little mad thing', a 'gross misconception, star-crossed waif, accusing ghost'. The birth of his daughter brings him relief from this fear: his main joy though is in the new relationship that the birth offers. He has now something, someone, to live for. It is a positive emotion, the first he has experienced in months. This joy in a new child and the hope which it brings is now consciously felt, but it is, for Rickie, sobered and diminished after his first happiness, because he remembers that his last child was by Dinah, his mistress, and that it had been born dead:

When about midnight, the eminent gynaecologist looked into the bookroom and said a girl, both splendid, he [Rickie] was pierced suddenly with such a pang of emotion that he could only grin and stammer like a schoolboy to hide his brimming eyes. A little later he went up to the dressing-room and saw, in a Moses basket on a stand, his daughter. The nurse returned to Madeleine and reported that he was as pleased as a dog with two tails: and a little later still when he went into the still ether-laden room to see his wife he kissed her and sat beside her bed with her hand in his; and they were both a little tearful, both delighted.

Undressing in the spare room, warily testing his heart for the first time in months, he decided that he felt different. *Better*. Hope had come back or life: perhaps they were the same thing. He had heard it said that nobody could go on living without any hope at all: he wondered for a long time whether it was true. He told himself that now he had a bit of something to live for, and promised his daughter love, and felt a stirring of tenderness and gratitude towards the mother.

He got into bed and lay on his back, his arms crossed behind his head, thinking of his luck, the fine, healthy offspring he had fathered. For the first time for months, Dinah's real face appeared, looking up at him calmly, one of her real faces. When she wore it, she had been lying under blankets in a high, narrow bed with an iron head-rail and looking most curiously complete and yet incomplete. Something had left her body yet was still informing it. With a sense of shock he told himself that his last child had been stillborn, his by Dinah.

Rickie's thoughts on the birth of his daughter are complicated by his emotional dilemma over the two sisters, yet, through the mix-up of divided loyalties, the realization of the importance of his new relationship with the child is a hopeful reality. Not all fictional husbands in modern novels share the heightened emotions of Lewis and Rickie. There is one at least who feels no primitive protective love, who has no desire to weep. There is no life-changing emotion for the husband in Evelyn Waugh's *Work Suspended*, 1941, when his first child is born; so completely lacking in any such emotion is he that he seeks reassurance from his friend Roger:

'It's extraordinary,' he said, 'I've got absolutely no feeling for this baby at all. I kept telling myself that when I saw, actually saw it, all manner of deep-seated atavistic emotions would come surging up. I was all set for a deep spiritual experience. They brought the thing in and showed it to me. I looked at it and waited and nothing at all happened. It was just like the first time one takes hashish—or being confirmed at school.'

'I knew a man who had five children,' I said; 'he felt just as you did until the fifth. Then he was suddenly overcome with love: he bought a thermometer and kept taking its temperature when the nurse was out of the room. I dare say it is a habit like hashish.'

'I don't feel as though I had anything to do with it. It's as though they showed me Lucy's appendix or a tooth they'd pulled out of her.'

'What's it like—I mean it isn't a freak or anything?'

'No, I've been into all that; two arms, two legs, one head, white—just a baby. Of course, you can't tell for some time whether it's sane or not.'

The majority of these twenty husbands from various novels written in the eighteenth, nineteenth and twentieth centuries feel miserable during the time in which they become fathers. Childbirth for most of these men is a time to be looked back on with anguish. No one course of conduct can guarantee a relaxed childbirth for a husband on this fictional evidence. Some pointers are revealed; apart from Fielding's Booth, who showed exceptional courage in staying behind his wife's pillow, even though it meant, as he said, that he underwent more pain in his body than she did in hers, it is not advisable to stay in the bedroom.

To do so is to risk semi-impotence or at least being screwed tightly in the 'vice of suffering'. Any other place is considered suitable—the dog's kennel or the floor outside the bedroom door. There is no precedent for husbands to be controlled or dignified during childbirth. If H. G. Wells's rationalist hero can cry shamelessly and even C. P. Snow's Lewis Eliot have smarting tear glands, to say nothing of the ravings and fainting fits of the nobleman in Clara Reeve's *The Two Mentors*, there is no need for any man to be afraid to show emotion.

From this group the modern husband, alone and purposeless, appears unfortunate by the side of the eighteenth-century husbands. They are shielded from unpleasant scenes, buoyed up with drinks and the company of friends, their minds untroubled by any guilt complexes over their wives' sufferings; they can relax with easy nerves. If they are the most obviously carefree the most obviously pitiful is the husband in Gissing's late nineteenth-century novel, poor Bob, who can only think of another child as another mouth to feed, and who thanks God when it dies. He is unable to feel what most of these fictional husbands and most of their wives do finally manage to feel—the joy of parenthood.

CHAPTER EIGHT

FROM CRYING OUT TO BEARING DOWN

WHILE I was collecting these descriptions, changes in manners during childbirth, from the eighteenth century until now, became easier to pick out from what I had formerly supposed to be an overall welter of sobs, groans and tearing pains; and from these, some generalized impressions emerged of the different attitudes towards childbirth in the three centuries.

The eighteenth century regarded childbirth, it seems, as a natural, frequent event involving all the community in which the mother lived. They recognized that it was an event which was likely to include death, which would require humour, endurance and good luck. In the childbirth scenes in these novels there are many characters, some giving advice and assisting at the birth, some coming in to chat, eat and drink: the atmosphere is convivial, busy and easy going. The women in labour are, for the most part, brave and practical. The husbands are well looked after; they reserve their love and any anxiety for their wives and mistresses and show little concern for the child. The doctors and midwives, with their free enterprise methods and their rivalry, have a bracing attitude to childbirth and, though the need for concealment and courage is not minimized, the most carefree illegitimate births come from this period.

In nineteenth-century novels childbirth is treated quite differently. These novels have the most unhappy, bleak confinements: deaths abound and are less casually treated than formerly. The impression is that childbirth is a difficult, secret, exclusively feminine affair. Anxieties have increased—fear of death, money

worries, the health, itself, of the women before and after childbirth, is more delicate and precarious. In this era illegitimate
births are tragedies; prostitutes who give birth easily and
comfortably have disappeared to be replaced by pure young
girls who are seduced with frightful consequences. A wife who
is about 'to cry out' has become a 'virtuous mother in the sacred
pangs of childbirth'.

By the middle of the twentieth century childbirth is no longer
sacred. The 'virtuous mother' is now being described as 'lying
almost naked, her tight knotted belly sticking up in a purple
lump, watching with fascination how it contracted and strained'.
The traditional womanly modesty is disappearing and docu-
mentary descriptions are being written. In these accounts the
doctors and midwives have been cleaned up and become antiseptic, respectable professionals. It is hard to imagine Mrs Gamp
or Dr Bangham as their predecessors. The baby has become
much more important both in embryo and at birth. It arouses
passionately strong paternal feelings in the sensitive husbands of
the twentieth century. There are fewer people involved in the
birth, which is now a more important and exclusive event in the
lives of both fictional parents.

In the light of these changes it becomes possible to chalk up a
few gains and losses for those of us who become parents today
outside of a novel. Now instead of lying in bed as I had done
thinking ruefully of the accuracy of Tolstoy's description of
childbirth, I could check our gains complacently by comparing
my lot with that of, for example, the Nun in *The Monk*, con-
soling myself for the hardness of the hospital bed with a reminder
that at least I was not giving birth in a crypt surrounded by the
decomposing dead. I could look up at the doctor and see, with
relief, that he was wearing a white coat and that his hands were
freshly scrubbed, that the midwife who assisted him was not
swigging gin or brandy or fanning me with a cabbage leaf. I
could reflect too that neither myself nor my child was likely to
die from childbed fever, and that I would be offered some sort of

analgesic and not just a bearing-down towel, hot milk or a vinegar-soaked bandage for my forehead.

These were gains. On the debit side I could expect a far less enjoyable pregnancy than those described in some eighteenth- or nineteenth-century novels. Instead of jaunting around the shops running up bills for baby clothes my only worry being how to make my husband pay for them all, or, as in nineteenth-century novels, lying on a couch, 'a delicate plant', quietly embroidering little caps; I would be given a 'list of necessities' from the hospital or midwife and checked and regimented throughout the nine months. I could no longer expect a crowd of women friends in the bedroom with me during the birth, and, if my baby's nose were squashed in the delivery, I could not hope that my doctor would cheerfully make a false bridge for it out of a whalebone from a woman's corset. Such losses as these were slight compared with the loss sustained by my husband. The poor choice offered to him, of either sitting outside or being in the bedroom during the birth and emerging semi-impotent, was even more terrible in view of those lost eighteenth-century confinement parties.

These losses caused by living in the twentieth century were, however, offset by my gain in the companionship provided by all those fictional wives and husbands who become mothers and fathers. No future confinement need be solitary and unfamiliar; indeed in their crowded company I had a good chance of enjoying being 'brought to bed'.

BIBLIOGRAPHY

An edition, in parentheses, subsequent to the one first listed, indicates the edition consulted by the author.

ALDINGTON, RICHARD: *Very Heaven*. Wm Heinemann, 1936.

ALLEN, WALTER: *All in a Lifetime*. Michael Joseph, 1959.

AUSTEN, JANE: *Sense and Sensibility*, 1811 (J. M. Dent & Sons, 1893); *Pride and Prejudice*, 1813 (J. M. Dent & Sons, 1893); *Mansfield Park*, 1814 (J. M. Dent & Sons, 1893); *Emma*, 1816 (J. M. Dent & Sons, 1893); *Northanger Abbey*, 1818 (J. M. Dent & Sons, 1893); *Persuasion*, 1818 (J. M. Dent & Sons, 1893).

BAGE, ROBERT: *Hermsprong*. Printed by Brett Smith for P. Wogan, P. Byrne, J. Moore and J. Rice. Dublin, 1796.

BAGNOLD, ENID: *The Squire*. Wm Heinemann, 1938.

BANKS, LYNNE REID: *The L-shaped Room*. Chatto & Windus, 1960.

BEHN, APHRA: *The Adventure of the Black Lady*, 1658. (Routledge & Sons, 1905.)

BRONTË, ANNE: *Agnes Grey*. Smith Elder, 1847; *The Tenant of Wildfell Hall*. Smith Elder, 1848.

BRONTË, CHARLOTTE: *Jane Eyre*. Smith Elder, 1847; *Shirley*. Smith Elder, 1849; *Villette*. Smith Elder, 1853.

BRONTË, EMILY: *Wuthering Heights*. Smith Elder, 1847.

BURNEY, FANNY: *Evelina*, 1778 (George Bell & Sons, 1882); *Cecilia*, 1782 (George Bell & Sons, 1882); *Camilla*, 1796. Printed for T. Payne at the Mews Gate, and T. Cadell Jun. & W. Davies (successors to Mr Cadell) in the Strand, London.

BUTLER, SAMUEL: *Erewhon* or *Over the Range*, 1872. (J. M. Dent & Sons, 1932.)

CRAIK, MRS DIANA MARY: *John Halifax, Gentleman*, 2 vols., 1856. (B. Tauchnitz, Leipzig, 1857.)

DEFOE, DANIEL: *Memoirs of a Cavalier*, 1720 (Shakespeare Head Edition, 1922); *The Fortunes and Misfortunes of Moll Flanders*, 1722 (Shakespeare Head Edition, 1922); *History of Colonel Jack*, 1722 (Shakespeare Head Edition, 1922); *The Fortunate Mistress* or *A History of Lady Roxana*, 1724 (Shakespeare Head Edition, 1922); *Complete Works*. Shakespeare Head Edition, 1922.

DICKENS, CHARLES: *Oliver Twist*, 1837–8 (J. M. Dent & Sons, 1906); *Barnaby Rudge*, 1840–1 (J. M. Dent & Sons, 1907); *Martin Chuzzlewit*, 1843–4 (J. M. Dent & Sons, 1907); *David Copperfield*, 1849–50 (J. M. Dent & Sons, 1908); *Little Dorrit*, 1855–7 (J. M. Dent & Sons, 1908); *Our Mutual Friend*, 1864–5 (J. M. Dent & Sons, 1908); *Complete Novels* (30 vols. Edited by R. Garnett. Chapman & Hall, 1900).

DISRAELI, BENJAMIN, 1ST EARL OF BEACONSFIELD: *Henrietta Temple*, 1837 (Peter Davies—The Brandenburg Edition of the Novels and Tales of the 1st Earl of Beaconsfield, 1927); *Sybil, or the Two Nations*, 1845 (Peter Davies—The Brandenburg Edition of the Novels and Tales of the 1st Earl of Beaconsfield, 1927).

EDGEWORTH, MARIA: *Leonora*, 1815 (Samuel H. Parker, 98 Washington Street, Boston. E. Littel, Philadelphia & Trenton, 1823–6); *Collected Works*. Samuel H. Parker, 98 Washington Street, Boston. E. Littel, Philadelphia & Trenton, 1823–6.

'ELIOT, GEORGE' (MARY ANN EVANS): *Scenes from Clerical Life*, 2 vols., 1858 (Oxford University Press, 1909); *Adam Bede*, 1859 (Zodiac Press, Chatto & Windus, 1950); *Middlemarch*, 1872 (Zodiac Press, Chatto & Windus, 1950); *Collected Works* (12 vols. Warwick Edition, Edinburgh, 1901–3).

FREUD, SIGMUND: *The Interpretation of Dreams*. Translated and edited by J. Strachey. Allen & Unwin, 1954.

FIELDING, HENRY: *Joseph Andrews*, 1742 (Blackwell—Shakespeare Head Edition, 1926); *The History of Jonathan Wild*, 1743 (Blackwell—Shakespeare Head Edition, 1926); *The History of Tom Jones, a Foundling*, 6 vols., 1849 (Blackwell—Shakespeare Head Edition, 1926); *Amelia*, 1752 (Blackwell—Shakespeare Head Edition, 1926); *Collected Novels*. Blackwell—Shakespeare Head Edition, 1926.

FORSTER, E. M.: *Where Angels Fear to Tread*. Wm Blackwood & Sons, 1905; *Howards End*. Edward Arnold, London and Putnam, New York, 1910.

GALSWORTHY, JOHN: *The Forsyte Saga*: vol. ii, *In Chancery*. Wm Heinemann, 1922; *The White Monkey*. Wm Heinemann, 1929.

GASKELL, MRS ELIZABETH CLEGHORN: *Mary Barton*, 1847 (World Classics Edition, Oxford University Press, 1906); *Ruth*, 1853 (World Classics Edition, Oxford University Press, 1909); *Sylvia's Lovers*, 1865 (World Classics Edition, Oxford University Press, 1909); *Wives and Daughters*, 1864 (Smith Elder, 1900); *Complete Novels* (World Classics Edition, Oxford University Press, 1906–9); *Life of Charlotte Brontë*, 2 vols., 1857 (Clement Shorter, Oxford, 1919).

GIBBONS, STELLA: *Cold Comfort Farm*. Longmans, 1932.

GISSING, GEORGE: *The Nether World*, 3 vols. (Smith Elder, 1889); *The Odd Women*, 3 vols., 1893 (Lawrence & Bullen, 1894); *In the Year of the Jubilee*, 3 vols. (Lawrence & Bullen, 1894).

GODWIN, WILLIAM: *Fleetwood*, 1805. (Richard Bentley, London; Bell & Bradford, Edinburgh; Cumming, Dublin and Galignan, Paris, 1832.)

GRAHAM, DR HARVEY: *Eternal Eve*. Wm Heinemann, 1950.

HARDY, THOMAS: *Tess of the D'Urbervilles*, 1891 (Wessex Edition, Macmillan & Co., 1912); *The Well-Beloved*, 1892 (Osgood, McIvaine & Co., 1897).

HUMPHREYS, EMYR: *A Man's Estate*. Eyre & Spottiswoode, 1955.

HUXLEY, ALDOUS: *Brave New World*. Chatto & Windus, 1932.

INCHBALD, MRS: *Nature and Art*, 2 vols. H. P. Rice, Philadephia, 1796.

JEROME, JEROME K.: *Three Men in a Boat*, 1889. (J. M. Dent & Sons, 1949.)

JOHNSON, PAMELA HANSFORD: *An Impossible Marriage*. Macmillan & Co., 1954; *The Unspeakable Skipton*. Macmillan & Co., 1959.

JOYCE, JAMES: *Ulysses*, 1922 (Printed in France, 1922. First printed in England, 1936. Pitman Press, Bath. John Lane, The Bodley Head, London, 1951.)

LAWRENCE, D. H.: *Sons and Lovers*, 1913 (Wm Heinemann, 1950); *The Rainbow*, 1915 (Wm Heinemann, 1950); *Women in Love*, 1922 (Wm Heinemann, 1950); *Lady Chatterley's Lover*. First published in Florence, 1928. First London edition, expurgated, 1928. (Penguin Edition, 1960.)

LEHMANN, ROSAMUND: *A Note in Music*. Chatto & Windus, 1930; *The Weather in the Streets*. Wm Collins, 1936; *Echoing Grove*. Wm Collins, 1953.

LESSING, DORIS: *A Proper Marriage*. Michael Joseph, 1954.

LEWIS, MATHEW GREGORY ('MONK'): *The Monk*, 1796. (Blue Ridge Mountain Press, 1952.)

MACKENZIE, COMPTON: *Carnival*. Martin Secker, 1912.

MEREDITH, GEORGE: *An Amazing Marriage*, 2 vols., 1895. Mickleham Edition of Meredith's Novels (18 vols.), 1922–4.

MITFORD, NANCY: *The Pursuit of Love*. Hamish Hamilton, 1945.

MOORE, GEORGE: *Muslin*, 1884 (Wm Heinemann, 1936); *A Mummer's Wife*, 1884 (Wm Heinemann, 1937); *Esther Waters*, 1920 (Wm Heinemann, 1937).

MORE, HANNAH: *The Two Wealthy Farmers* or *The History of Mr Bragwell*, 1795. (From *The Complete Works of Hannah More*, London. Printed by A. Straham for T. Cadell, Jun. & G. W. Davies in the Strand, 1807.)

MORTIMER, PENELOPE: *Daddy's Gone a-Hunting*. Michael Joseph, 1959.

OPIE, MRS AMELIA: *Father and Daughter* or *Father and Daughter and Temper*, 1801 (Brown, Green & Longmans, 1843); *Adeline Mowbray* or *The Mother and Daughter*, 1804 (Printed for Longmans, Hurst, Rees & Orme, London and Constable & Co., Edinburgh, 1805); *Madeline*, 2 vols., 1822 (Printed for Longmans, Hurst, Rees & Orme, London and Constable & Co., Edinburgh, 1823).

READ, DR GRANTLEY DICK: *Childbirth without Fear*, 1942. (Wm Heinemann, Medical Series. Revised Edition, 1954.)

REEVE, CLARA: *The Two Mentors*, 1783. (Printed for J. Mawman, Poultry, London, 1803. Third Edition.)

RICHARDSON, SAMUEL: *Pamela*, 1740 (Chapman & Hall, 1902); *Sir Charles Grandison*, 1753–4 (Chapman & Hall, 1902).

SCOTT, SIR WALTER: *Guy Mannering*, 1815 (Adam & Charles Black, 1895); *The Antiquary*, 1816 (Adam & Charles Black, 1895); *The Heart of Midlothian*, 1818 (Adam & Charles Black, 1895); *Kenilworth*, 1821 (Adam & Charles Black, 1895); *The Pirate*, 1821 (Adam & Charles Black, 1895); *Redgauntlet*, 1824 (Adam & Charles Black, 1895); *St Ronan's Well*, 1824 (Adam & Charles Black, 1895).

SHELLEY, MARY WOLLSTONECRAFT: *Frankenstein* or *The Modern Prometheus*. H. Colburn & R. Bentley, 1831.

SMITH, CHARLOTTE: *Count de St Geran*, from *The Romances of Real Life*. 3 vols. Translated from the French of Guy de Pitaval. T. Cadell, 1787; *Emmeline* or *The Orphan of the Castle*. 4 vols. T. Cadell, 1789, Third Edition; *The Young Philosopher*. 4 vols. T. Cadell, 1798.

SMOLLETT, TOBIAS: *The Adventures of Roderick Random*, 2 vols., 1748 (Blackwell—Shakespeare Head Edition, 1925); *The Adventures of Peregrine Pickle*, 4 vols., 1751 (Blackwell—Shakespeare Head Edition, 1925).

SNOW, C. P.: *Homecomings*. Macmillan & Co., 1959.

STERNE, LAURENCE: *The Life and Opinions of Tristram Shandy*, 9 vols., 1760–8. (John Lehmann Chiltern Edition, 1948.)

TAYLOR, ELIZABETH: *A View of the Harbour*. Peter Davies, 1947; *Sleeping Beauty*. Peter Davies, 1953.

THACKERAY, WILLIAM MAKEPEACE: *Vanity Fair*, 1847. (The Oxford Library, Chilworth, 1891.)

TROLLOPE, ANTHONY: *Doctor Thorne*, 3 vols., 1858. (Harper & Bros., New York, 1958.)

WAUGH, EVELYN: *Work Suspended*. Chapman & Hall, 1941; *Brideshead Revisited*. Chapman & Hall, 1945.

WELLS, H. G.: *Marriage*. Macmillan & Co., 1912.

WEST, REBECCA: *The Judge*. Hutchinson, 1916.

WHITE, ANTONIA: *The Lost Traveller*. Eyre & Spottiswoode, 1950.

WOOLF, VIRGINIA: *Orlando*, 1928 (Hogarth Press. Uniform Edition, 1933); *Flush* (Hogarth Press. Uniform Edition, 1933).

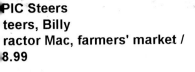

TRACTOR MAC

CERTIFICATE OF REGISTRATION

• • •

This book belongs to

_____